LIFE ON THE MALECÓN

The Rutgers Series in Childhood Studies

The Rutgers Series in Childhood Studies is dedicated to increasing our understanding of children and childhoods, past and present, throughout the world. Children's voices and experiences are central. Authors come from a variety of fields, including anthropology, criminal justice, history, literature, psychology, religion, and sociology. The books in this series are intended for students, scholars, practitioners, and those who formulate policies that affect children's everyday lives and futures.

Edited by Myra Bluebond-Langner, Board of Governors Professor of Anthropology, Rutgers University and True Colours Chair in Palliative Care for Children and Young People, University College London, Institute of Child Health.

Advisory Board

Perri Klass, *New York University*
Jill Korbin, *Case Western Reserve University*
Bambi Schieffelin, *New York University*
Enid Schildkraut, *American Museum of Natural History
and Museum for African Art*

Worship in 1 Corinthians 12–14

When the Corinthians became believers, they had a profound experience of the Holy Spirit working within them, which greatly enriched their community, so that they are not lacking in any "charism," any spiritual gift (1:7; 12:1). These spiritual gifts included a variety of activities—speaking a word of wisdom or of knowledge, expressions of faith, the ability to heal, speaking the word of God by prophesying, determining what is true or false prophecy by the discernment of spirits, speaking in unintelligible tongues as a way of praising God, and the ability to interpret the meaning of what is spoken in tongues (12:8–10). These spiritual gifts were exercised within the liturgical assembly to enhance the worship of the community. Indeed, "to each is given the manifestation of the Spirit for some benefit" (12:7). Paul needs to instruct the Corinthians regarding these spiritual gifts, since the exercise of such a rich variety of spiritual activities could be chaotic rather than beneficial for their worship.

First of all, Paul lays down a fundamental criterion for how the Corinthians can determine whether or not someone exercising a spiritual gift is truly speaking in the Spirit, and thus benefiting the worship of the assembly. No one speaking in the Spirit of God can possibly say anything as detrimental as "Jesus is cursed," and no one can say something as beneficial as "Jesus is Lord," except in the Holy Spirit (12:3). The same Spirit, Lord, and God produces these different spiritual activities (12:4–6, 11).

The exercise of each spiritual gift has an essential role to play in edifying or benefiting the worship of the assembly as the one body of Christ (12:12–30; 10:17). Consequently, the various attributes of Christian love are absolutely necessary for the harmonious performance of these quite different spiritual activities during worship. For example, as Paul poetically and eloquently elucidates, "love is patient, love is kind," allowing each individual to exercise his or her particular spiritual gift. One with this kind of love is not envious of another's spiritual gift, nor boastful or arrogant of one's own spiritual gift (13:4). The Corinthians are to pursue this kind of love to ensure that everyone is

also alludes to the community as the body of Christ. People who do not recognize the community as the body of the Lord but dare to eat the bread and drink the cup bring judgment upon themselves" (Collins, *First Corinthians*, 439). See also Mitchell, "Paul's Eucharistic Theology," 250–62.

able to exercise his or her spiritual gift for the good of the worshiping assembly.[25]

Although all of the spiritual gifts have a distinct role to play, some are more beneficial than others for communal worship. In particular, Paul urges the Corinthians to place a higher value on the spiritual gift of prophesying, which makes the word of God relevant for the lives of those in the worshiping assembly, than of speaking in unintelligible tongues. The one speaking in tongues does not speak to human beings but to God, for no one listens, as he is speaking mysteries by the Spirit. But one who prophesies speaks edification and encouragement and consolation to human beings. One speaking in a tongue builds up oneself, but one prophesying builds up the assembly (14:1–4).[26]

Therefore, one speaking in a tongue should pray that he may interpret. For if one prays in a tongue, his spirit prays, but his mind is unproductive. One who prays with his spirit should also pray with his mind; one who sings praise with his spirit should also sing praise with his mind. No one can respond with a liturgical "amen" to what is unintelligible; it does not build up others (14:13–17).[27] But if all prophesy, an unbeliever who enters the assembly will fall down and worship God, declaring, "God is really among you!" (14:24–25), a confessional exclamation indicating a conversion to faith in and worship of the one and only true God based on an authentic manifestation that God is "really" present in this worshiping assembly.[28]

25. "While praising love, Paul is blaming the Corinthians at the same time. The upshot is that although the gifts of the Spirit are conspicuous in their assembly, their lack of love is even more conspicuous. Rather than being a hymn glorifying how wonderful love is, this text becomes a subtle commentary on what is rotten in Corinth" (Garland, *1 Corinthians*, 616–17).

26. "Just as the foundational gift of love builds up the church (8:1), so the exercise of the individual charisms, the active expressions of love, builds up the church. Among the charisms the exercise of the gift of prophecy particularly contributes to the building up of the church. An authentic charism, prophecy is a manifestation of the Spirit that builds up the church" (Collins, *First Corinthians*, 493).

27. "The criterion governing Paul's conclusion is what will do the most good for the community. Public worship is for mutual edification not private enrichment" (Garland, *1 Corinthians*, 643).

28. Sandnes, "Prophecy," 1–15. "In all *reality* they encounter not simply human religion which constructs or projects a god; they encounter *God*, who draws forth authentic worship as he is authentically active and present among the believers" (Thiselton, *Corinthians*, 1130).

When the Corinthians assemble for worship, each spiritual activity—a psalm, a teaching, a revelation, a tongue, an interpretation—should be exercised in an orderly way for building up. If anyone speaks in a tongue, it should be two, or at most three, each in turn, and someone must interpret. If there is no interpreter, a speaker in tongues should be silent in the assembly. Let him speak privately to himself and to God. Two or three prophets may speak in the assembly, and the others discern. They can all prophesy one by one, so that all may learn and all may be encouraged (14:26–31). They should strive to prophesy and not forbid speaking in tongues. But everything must be done properly and in order (14:39–40). Paul thus teaches the Corinthians and all of us that communal worship should not only praise God but also build up one another.[29]

Worship in 1 Corinthians 15–16

In concluding his detailed discourse on the resurrection of Christ (15:1–54a), Paul leads the Corinthians, gathered as a liturgical assembly, in an act of worship that celebrates the significance of what God has done in raising Jesus from the dead. First, he introduces a scriptural quotation, which combines Isa 25:8a and Hos 13:14b, with the assertion, "Then will come to be the word that is written" (15:54b). This prepares his audience to hear a "word" or "saying" written in the past with a scriptural authority that remains valid for the present, as expressed by the perfect tense of the Greek participle "written" (*gegrammenos*). That it "will come to be" assures the Corinthians of its certain fulfillment in the future, based on its authority as God's scriptural "word" of prophecy. Paul will thus exemplify how the exercise of prophecy in the worshiping assembly builds up and benefits the Corinthian community as the body of Christ (14:1–4).

The scriptural word of prophecy commences the celebratory worship of what God has accomplished with the proclamation, "Death is

29. "What is imperative is that when the community comes together for worship, the order in the assembly should reflect the order that exists within the body of Christ. Everything is to be done with propriety and in order" (Collins, *First Corinthians*, 517). "Paul states the overarching principle that should govern the expression of spiritual phenomena in worship. Everything must be done in an orderly manner" (Garland, *1 Corinthians*, 674).

swallowed up in victory!" (Isa 25:8a in 15:54b). In accord with Jewish apocalyptic eschatology, here "death," literally, "the death" (*ho thanatos*), is regarded as a personified cosmic power that is God's last enemy (cf. 15:26) or opponent in the great eschatological battle for ultimate control over all of creation.[30] That death "is swallowed up" by God (divine passive) in the manner that a wild animal completely consumes its prey or the waves of the sea drown something so that it disappears assures the audience of death's utter destruction and disappearance, rendering it powerless. Ironically, the death that swallows and devours the living is itself swallowed up by the living God. That death is swallowed up by God "in victory" assures the Corinthians that God will be the victor in the great eschatological battle and ultimately triumph over the cosmic power of death. Paul's proclamation of this scriptural prophecy thus leads the Corinthians in a hymnic praise of the grace of God.

This epistolary act of worship continues, as the second part of the scriptural "word" of prophecy draws the audience into a taunting interrogation of the personified power of death by means of a parallel pair of penetrating rhetorical questions: "Where, O death, is *your* victory? Where, O death, is *your* sting?" (Hos 13:14b in 15:55). Since the inimical power of death will ultimately be swallowed up and completely defeated in God's victory (15:54b), the first question, with its emphasis upon the pronoun "your" and taunting direct address of a personified "death," mocks any claim death may think it has to "the victory."[31] In contrast to *God's* complete victory over death, "Where, O death, is *your* victory?" (15:55a). As the Corinthians realize that the implied answer is absolutely "nowhere!," by such taunting they are celebrating the grace of God's ultimate defeat of the cosmic power of death over them.

The celebratory worship of the Corinthians includes a second taunting question, "Where, O death, is *your* sting?" (15:55b), which reinforces and develops the rhetorical impact of the first taunting question (15:55a). In contrast to *God's* overwhelming and complete "swallowing up" of the inimical power of death, the question mocks a personified death by asking where is "the sting" that is *yours*? Not only

30. de Boer, *Defeat of Death*; Gillman, "Thematic Comparison," 439–54.

31. "To press home the powerlessness of death to damage, to intimidate, or dismay, Paul uses the vocative of address as a *taunt*, like a taunt to a hostile but disarmed, bound, and powerless attacker" (Thiselton, *Corinthians*, 1301).

can death no longer swallow up the living because it has itself been swallowed up, but it no longer has any "sting" to harm the living, in the manner of the poisonous sting of a wild animal. Thus, by all of this taunting, the Corinthians are celebrating that not only will death have no claim to final victory over them (15:55a), but it will ultimately have no power ("sting") to harm them (15:55b).

By then asserting that "the sting of death is sin and the power of sin is the law" (15:56), Paul shifts the attention of his Corinthian audience from the scriptural quote's future taunting of death at the end when death is swallowed up in victory to the still-present menace through sin of the enemy that is death. Death as an apocalyptic power uses another apocalyptic power, sin, as its instrument to inject the poisonous "sting" that brings about death. This reminds the audience that the death that came from the first human, Adam (15:21–22), was a result of his sin (Gen 2:17; 3:6, 19). Though they may look forward in confident hope and already celebrate as a worshiping assembly the scripture quote's future taunting of death's "sting," the Corinthians and all of us still experience the death-bringing "sting" of the power of sin (6:18; 7:28; 8:12; 15:3, 17, 34) through the law (9:8–9, 20; 14:21, 34) that makes sin a reality in the lives of human beings.[32]

Although we still experience the "sting" of death through our sins (15:56), Paul, as he continues this epistolary act of worship, leads his Corinthian congregation in an exuberant exclamation of thanksgiving that acknowledges and pays tribute to the grace of God, "But thanks (literally, 'grace' [*charis*]) to God who gives us the victory through our Lord Jesus Christ!" (15:57). The scriptural quote's future "victory" when "death is swallowed up in victory!" (15:54b) is given as a gift of God's grace to "us"—Paul, his audience, and all believers—through our Lord Jesus Christ, the one who died for our sins (15:3) and was raised from the dead so that we are no longer in our sins (15:17), the sins that inject us with the poisonous "sting" of death. That we have been given as a gift of the grace of God "the victory," that *the* victory over death as the last enemy (15:26) is *ours* because of the grace of God, intensifies the

---

32. "Death injects mortality in man, and the means by which it does so is sin. . . . According to Paul, there is a clear connection between death and sin, between the power of death and the power of sin, both being active in the life of mankind" (Hollander and Holleman, "1 Cor 15:56," 277).

celebratory worship of the scriptural quote's taunt—"Where, O death, is *your* victory?" (15:55a).[33]

Paul then extends this celebratory liturgical worship to the Corinthians' ethical worship in their lives outside of the assembly. He exhorts his Corinthian congregation to "become firm, unmovable, abounding in the work of the Lord always, knowing that your labor is not in vain in the Lord" (15:58). They can be assured that their labor is not in vain in the *Lord*, so that they may abound in the work of the *Lord*, because it is through the resurrection of the *Lord* Jesus Christ that they and all believers are given "*the* victory" as a gift of God's grace. That the victory over death belongs to the congregation ensures that their work (cf. 3:13–15; 9:1) and labor (cf. 3:8) in bringing others to faith and living it themselves is not "in vain" or "empty" in the Lord. On the contrary, it is part of their ethical worship as those who call upon the name of our *Lord* Jesus Christ when they are gathered together as a liturgical assembly (1:2). It is part of the worship that builds up the community as the body of Christ.[34]

As the letter comes to a close, Paul directs the Corinthians, whose worship he has been leading and instructing as they listened to the letter in their liturgical assembly, to greet one another with a "holy kiss," a gesture expressive of fraternal affection and unity appropriate for the worshiping congregation (16:20). Before the final greeting and after Paul's warning that if anyone does not love the Lord, let him be ac-

---

33. On 15:57, Thiselton (*Corinthians*, 1303–4) points out, "Here is a classic illocutionary speech-act (an act performed *in* the saying of an utterance): Paul gives thanks for the gracious gift of victory over death and over death's empowerment by sin and by the law in alliance. It is an *act* of thanksgiving; a verbal equivalent to throwing one's arms around someone in gratitude; or like throwing one's hat in the air *in sheer exultation*. . . . [E]ven if the last resurrection is still future, the basis of the victory is a present gift, providing grounds for present exultation and thanksgiving. It is not a mere present of future certainty about resurrection; it also expresses the present gift of grace to believers for whom the destructive potential of sin, the law, and death as a terrifying prospect has been broken. The present reality is that the sting of death has been drawn out by Christ's victory. Believers already in some measure share in this victory, even though the final appropriation of all that this entails has yet to be appropriated and experienced fully at the last day" (emphasis original).

34. "In Paul's rhetorical lexis 'work' and 'toil' are almost technical terms used to describe the work of evangelization. On the 'work' of the Corinthians see 3:10–17. It is a work of building up the community" (Collins, *First Corinthians*, 583). On 1 Cor 15:54–58, see Heil, *1 Corinthians*, 247–60.

cursed, Paul leads the congregation in a terse eschatological prayer in Aramaic, "*marana tha*," that is, "Our Lord, come!" (16:22). Paul together with the Corinthians thus ardently pray for the final coming of our Lord Jesus Christ to bring the salvation they have begun to experience to its glorious completion.[35]

Paul's verbless double greeting that closes the letter functions as a concise yet comprehensive summary of what the Corinthians have experienced in listening to the letter as a speech act: "The grace of the Lord Jesus has been, is, and will be with you" (16:23) and "my love has been, is, and will be with all of you in Christ Jesus!" (16:24). The "grace" (*charis*) of the Lord Jesus and the communal "love" (*apagē*) in Christ Jesus complement one another as key terms associated with both the liturgical and ethical worship that has been expressed throughout the preceding letter. Indeed, it is within the dynamic domain of being "in Christ Jesus" as a result of divine grace that Christian love is evident and operative as a correspondence to this grace that comes from the "Lord Jesus" to the Corinthians gathered together for worship in the name of the Lord Jesus Christ (1:2, 10; 5:4; 6:11).

The verbless greeting of "the grace of the Lord Jesus with you" (16:23) recalls and reinforces that the collection for the Christians in Jerusalem is a gracious gift, literally a "grace," in appreciative recognition that the grace of the Lord Jesus has its origin in the mother church of Jerusalem (16:3). It resonates with and corresponds to the thankful acclamation of "grace" to the God who gives us the victory over death through our Lord Jesus Christ (15:57), to the "grace" that enabled Paul to labor abundantly as the least of the apostles (15:10), to the "grace" by which one thanks God for a meal (10:30), and to the "grace" given

35. On the Aramaic formula, *marana tha*, here, Fee (*Corinthians*, 838) writes, "its use in a context like this can only be explained on the basis of its prior use in the Aramaic-speaking church, almost certainly in the context of worship. Whether or not it belonged to the 'liturgy' of the Lord's Table in such an early setting is moot. If so, then it probably meant 'Come, O Lord,' and is to be understood as an early eschatological prayer, similar to that in Rev. 22:20, 'Come, Lord Jesus.'" "In fact it has often been claimed that the finale of Paul's letter, beginning with his mention of the holy kiss in v. 20, served as a transition between the reading of the letter and the celebration of Eucharist. The autograph of 16:21 is certainly an epistolary formula. The holy kiss, the formulae of inclusion and exclusion, and a grace benediction are, however, similar to phenomena found in the liturgy of the early church. . . . The manifold references to the Eucharist throughout the letter clearly portray the Corinthian community as a eucharistic community" (Collins, *First Corinthians*, 615).

to Paul to lay the foundation for the Corinthian community (3:10). It also resonates and corresponds to the "grace" given to the Corinthians in Christ Jesus (1:4), so that they are not lacking in any "charism," any specific manifestation of "grace" (1:7). And this final greeting of "grace," together with the initial greeting of "grace" and peace from God our Father and the Lord Jesus Christ (1:3), form a literary inclusion that places the entire letter within a framework that reminds the Corinthians of the divine grace they have already received. It communicates to them a renewed experience of that grace as they listen to the letter, and it prepares them for future experiences of that grace.[36]

This final greeting of grace is intensified and complemented by Paul's very personal greeting—"my love with all of you in Christ Jesus" (16:24). As Paul's personal example of how everything they do should be done "in love" (16:14), it is a final reminder to the Corinthians of how Christian "love" is to accompany the manifestations of divine "grace" within their communal worship. They are to pursue the "love" that must be demonstrated toward one another as they exercise their spiritual gifts, their individual gifts of grace, especially prophesying, in their liturgical assembly (14:1). This "love" is even greater than faith and hope (13:13). "Love" never fails (13:8). "Love" is patient and kind (13:4), and without "love" anything they might accomplish is meaningless (13:1–3). This is the kind of "love" that builds up their community as the body of Christ (8:1). And finally, this assurance of Paul's "love" for *all* of the Corinthians as a unified community that he founded as their "father" (4:15) bolsters his expressed desire to come to them, not with a disciplinary rod to correct the divisive rivalries that have arisen among them, but in "love" with a Spirit of gentleness (4:21).[37]

---

36. "Grace is the beginning and the end of the Christian gospel; it is the single word that most fully expresses what God has done and will do for his people in Christ Jesus" (Fee, *Corinthians*, 839). With regard to this final greeting of grace, Thiselton (*Corinthians*, 1352) states that it "may add further weight to the view that Paul expects his letter to be read aloud to the church assembled, probably for worship. Grace marks this epistle from one end (1:1–3) to the other (16:21–24)."

37. On "Spirit of gentleness" here, Fee (*God's Empowering Presence*, 121) says, "even though the emphasis here lies on 'attitude,' the very expression implies the presence of the Spirit who produces such an attitude in Paul." "In 1 Corinthians Paul's last word to the community reprises the theme of love that had pervaded much of the letter. The motif of universal love provides an *inclusio* for Paul's final greetings (16:13–24). 'All' and 'love' appear in both v. 14 and v. 24. Verse 14 emphasizes the comprehensive

Conclusion: Worship in 1 Corinthians

To sum up, after his opening greeting of "grace" (1:3) to the Corinthians gathered for worship as those who call upon the name of our Lord Jesus Christ (1:2), Paul initiated the ritualistic worship in the letter with a thanksgiving to God for the grace the Corinthians have already received (1:4). The rivalries that have arisen in the Corinthian community (1:10–11) contradict and threaten to destroy their status as the holy temple (3:16–17) that offers proper liturgical and ethical worship to God.

When the Corinthians are gathered together as a worshiping assembly, they are to carry out and complete Paul's ritualistic pronouncement of judgment on the incestuous member of the community (5:1) with their own performance of a ritualistic act (5:4b). They are to publicly and officially expel him from the community and send him out into the profane world as a ceremonial ritual that purifies them for proper worship as the holy temple of God (5:5). They then may celebrate a new feast of Passover liturgically in the Eucharist and ethically in their moral lives as Christians (5:7–8). They are thus to avoid sexual immorality, since the sexually immoral individual sins against both his individual and corporate body (6:18), rendering both of these bodies incapable of the worship that glorifies God. Not only does an unbelieving spouse not defile or disqualify the worship of a believing spouse, but, because the whole family has been rendered "holy" (7:12–14), all of its members, spouses as well as children, may participate in both the liturgical and ethical worship appropriate to the Corinthian church as God's holy temple.

By their eating and drinking at the Eucharist celebrated within their worshiping assembly, without also eating the food sacrificed to demonic idols outside of their assembly, the Corinthians will give glory to and properly worship God both liturgically and ethically (1 Corinthians 8–10). Men and women are to wear the hairstyles proper to their gender out of respect for themselves as individuals (11:4, 5–6, 13, 14, 15), for one another as men and women (11:8–9, 11–12), for the other churches (11:16), and for the angels (11:10), Christ (11:3),

---

nature of universal Christian love; v. 24 expresses its personal nature. As Paul extends his love to all members of the community his words serve as a final reminder that there should be no divisions within that community" (Collins, *First Corinthians*, 616).

and God (11:3, 7, 12). They must include the practice of this custom in their liturgical gatherings in order to worship God properly by doing everything for the glory of God (10:31). Those individuals who go ahead with their own suppers before the Lord's Supper contradict the communal unity of the participants that is its very purpose. Therefore, Paul urges the Corinthians that when they come together to eat, they are to wait for and welcome one another into this communal coming together for their eucharistic worship (11:20–34).

The Corinthians are to practice the Christian love that ensures that everyone in the community is able to exercise his or her spiritual gift for the good of the worshiping assembly (1 Corinthians 12–13). Although all of the spiritual gifts have a distinct role to play, some are more beneficial than others for communal worship. In particular, Paul urges the Corinthians to place a higher value on the spiritual gift of prophesying, which makes the word of God relevant to the worshiping assembly. The one who prophesies speaks edification and encouragement and consolation to human beings. Paul thus teaches the Corinthians and all of us that communal worship should not only praise God but build up one another (1 Corinthians 14).

Paul leads his Corinthian congregation in an exuberant exclamation of thanksgiving that acknowledges and pays tribute to the grace of God: "But thanks/grace to God who gives us the victory through our Lord Jesus Christ!" (15:57). The future "victory" when "death is swallowed up in victory!" (15:54b) is given as a gift of God's grace to "us"—Paul, his audience, and all believers—through our Lord Jesus Christ, the one who died for our sins (15:3) and was raised from the dead so that we are no longer in our sins (15:17), the sins that inject us with the poisonous "sting" of death (15:56). That we have been given as a gift of the grace of God "the victory," that *the* victory over death as the last enemy (15:26) is *ours* because of the grace of God, intensifies the celebratory worship of the scriptural taunt—"Where, O death, is *your* victory?" (15:55a).

Before the final greeting and after Paul's warning that if anyone does not love the Lord, let him be accursed, Paul leads the congregation in a fervent eschatological prayer, "Our Lord, come!" (16:22). Paul together with the Corinthians thus ardently pray for the final coming of our Lord Jesus Christ to bring the salvation they have begun to experience to its glorious completion.

Finally, Paul's verbless double greeting that closes the letter functions as a concise yet comprehensive summary of what the Corinthians have experienced in listening to the letter as a speech act: "The grace of the Lord Jesus has been, is, and will be with you" (16:23) and "my love has been, is, and will be with all of you in Christ Jesus!" (16:24). The "grace" of the Lord Jesus and the communal "love" in Christ Jesus complement one another as key terms associated with both the liturgical and ethical worship that has been expressed throughout the preceding letter. Indeed, it is within the dynamic domain of being "in Christ Jesus" as a result of divine grace that Christian love is evident and operative as a correspondence to this grace that comes from the "Lord Jesus" for the Corinthians gathered together for worship in the name of the Lord Jesus Christ (1:2, 10; 5:4; 6:11).

2 Corinthians

Circumstances both within the Corinthian community and with regard to Paul's apostolic ministry led him to change his original travel plans (1 Cor 16:3–9) for his next visit to Corinth. These circumstances apparently caused some misunderstandings of Paul on the part of the Corinthians, so that their relationship was seriously affected. Paul, probably from Macedonia, writes this second letter to the Corinthians for three primary purposes. First, he informs the Corinthians of his joy and confidence in them in light of their present reconciliation with God, Paul, and one another regarding the change in his travel plans to visit them (2 Cor 1–7). Second, having restored his relationship with the Corinthians, Paul urges them to complete their collection for the Christians at Jerusalem (1 Cor 16:1–2) before Paul's next visit to them (2 Cor 8–9). And third, having mentioned his intention to come to them, Paul prepares them for his visit by providing them with criteria for distinguishing between the deceitfulness of the rival apostles opposed to him and the genuineness of his own apostleship (2 Cor 10–13).[1]

2 Corinthians as a Ritual of Worship

Worship in 2 Corinthians 1–7

Paul, as an apostle of Christ Jesus through the will of God, together with Timothy, addresses the Corinthians as "the church of God which is in Corinth together with all the holy ones who are in the whole of Achaia" (1:1). The Corinthians are associated with all of the other believers in

---

1. Harris, *Corinthians*, 51–52; Stegman, *Second Corinthians*, 15–27.

Achaia, the Roman province where the city of Corinth is located, as those who have been made "holy ones" by God because of what God has done for them in Christ Jesus. As "the holy ones" (*tois hagiois*), they are separated from the evil in the world as those consecrated for service to God, which includes both their liturgical and ethical worship, as the "church," the "assembly" (*ekklēsia*), of God.[2]

With the verbless epistolary greeting of "grace to you and peace from God our Father and the Lord Jesus Christ" (1:2), Paul initiates the ritualistic worship of this letter. His greeting reminds his Corinthian audience of the grace and peace they have already received when they became believers. These are the divine gifts that motivate their worship. The greeting also prepares them for a renewed experience of this divine grace and peace as they now listen to the letter as a liturgical assembly. And it expresses Paul's prayer that in the future they may continue to experience this divine grace and peace, after and as a result of having listened to this letter from Paul, as an apostle of Christ Jesus through the will of God (1:1).[3]

With a liturgical benediction, "Blessed (*eulogētos*) the God and Father of our Lord Jesus Christ, the Father of mercies and the God of all encouragement" (1:3), Paul leads the Corinthian congregation in a communal act of worship that praises God.[4] Having no explicit verb, the

2. "Paul's thinking on holiness is primarily communal. Although each person who belongs to Jesus Christ belongs to him personally, there is nothing individualistic about such relationship. As such, it is the church, collectively, that is called to holy living, the individual only being important as a constituent member of the community. In 2 Cor 1:1, the word *hagioi* is closely linked with *ekklēsia*. To be a 'member of the church' then would be equivalent to 'being a holy one,' in which case it might be appropriate to translate both simply as the 'people of God'" (Adewuya, "Holiness in 2 Corinthians," 204).

3. Commenting on the greeting in 1:2, Harris (*Corinthians*, 135) states, "Paul's wish for the Corinthians in effect constitutes a prayer for them."

4. With regard to the word "blessed," Patsch ("*eulogeō*," 80) notes, "It belongs to a doxological type of expression that is derived from an OT and Jewish traditional form of prayer. In the NT it always refers to God." "In most of Paul's letters a brief prayer of thanksgiving follows the greeting, but in 2 Corinthians Paul makes use of a benediction rather than a thanksgiving in order to praise God. Although both thanksgivings and benedictions are prayers, the benediction has a more liturgical tone" (Matera, *II Corinthians*, 40). The Greek word translated as "encouragement" (*paraklēsis*) here also has connotations of "comfort" and "consolation" (see BDAG, 766).

benediction can be understood as "blessed be" and/or "blessed is" God.[5] The communal dimension, as indicated by the inclusive first-person plural pronoun in the reference to "our" Lord Jesus Christ, continues with the description of God as the one who encourages "us"—Paul, the Corinthians, and all believers—in "our" every affliction so that "we" are able to encourage those in every affliction through the encouragement with which "we ourselves" are encouraged by God, for as the sufferings of Christ abound toward "us," so through Christ abounds also "our" encouragement (1:4–5).

Even when Paul shifts to the use of the first-person plural to refer primarily to himself, he does so in a way that continues to draw his Corinthian audience into a close relationship with him in their mutual and communal praise of God as the source of all encouragement (1:3): "If we are afflicted, it is for your encouragement and salvation; if we are encouraged, it is for your encouragement which becomes effective in the endurance of the same sufferings which we also suffer, and our hope for you is firm, knowing that as you are sharers of the sufferings, so also of the encouragement" (1:6–7).[6]

After informing the Corinthians that God rescued him from a great danger of death in the province of Asia, Paul expresses his hope that God will rescue him again (1:10). And with the cooperation of the Corinthians such a divine rescue will result in their participation in a widespread worship of God on behalf of Paul. If the Corinthians join together in helping with prayer on behalf of Paul, then the divine gift of rescue that will be given to Paul through many prayers will result in many persons giving thanks to God on behalf of Paul (1:11).[7]

---

5. In reference to this benediction Harris *(Corinthians,* 141) comments that whether it "expresses a wish that God be praised or affirms that God is worthy of praise, the very wish or affirmation amounts to praise or thanksgiving. That is, doxology is an indirect expression of gratitude."

6. "Paul is alluding to *Christ's* sufferings and *God's* comfort. . . . it was not simply a matter of Corinthian suffering followed automatically and directly by divine comfort, but rather of Paul's mediating God's comfort to the Corinthians in their suffering" (Harris, *Corinthians,* 150).

7. According to Matera *(II Corinthians,* 44), Paul "concludes his benediction by calling upon the Corinthians to join with others in giving thanks for the gifts bestowed upon him, thereby uniting them with a chorus of people who are already thanking God for rescuing the apostle."

The change in Paul's itinerary for his next visit to the Corinthians raises the question of the reliability of his word (1:17). But he assures his audience that his reliability is rooted in the faithfulness of God as proclaimed in the word of the gospel about Jesus Christ. For the Son of God, Jesus Christ, who was proclaimed by Paul, Silvanus, and Timothy, was completely reliable (1:18-19). For, as many as are the promises of God, the totally reliable and faithful "yes" to them is in Jesus Christ; therefore, indeed it is through him that the liturgical "amen" to God for glory goes through "us"—not only Paul, Silvanus, and Timothy but by implication the Corinthians and all believers as well (1:20). In other words, Jesus Christ, in whom is the faithful and reliable "yes" to God's promises, not only motivates but mediates the worship of believers. It is "through" Christ that the liturgical "amen" acknowledging and confirming the faithfulness of God in the worship that gives glory to God goes "through" us.[8]

As indicated by the introductory greeting of "grace to you and peace from God our Father and the Lord Jesus Christ" (1:2), "grace" is a gift that comes from God. It is by the "grace" that comes from God that Paul conducts himself not only in the world but especially toward the Corinthians (1:12). It would have been a double "grace" from God (1:15), if Paul had been able to visit the Corinthians both on his way to and from Macedonia (1:16). But "grace" is also a word used to thank God in acknowledgement of the grace that comes as a gift from God. And so Paul proclaims, "thanks," literally "grace" (*charis*), to God, "who always leads us in triumph in Christ and manifests the fragrance of the knowledge of him through us in every place" (2:14). While "us" here refers primarily to Paul, it has an inclusive edge implying that God is always leading not only Paul but the Corinthians and all of "us" believers in triumph in Christ, and manifesting the fragrance of the knowledge of Christ in every place through not only Paul but the Corinthians and all of "us" believers. Consequently, Paul here is inviting his Corinthian

---

8. "[I]f divine promises, whatever their number, are realized in and through Christ (v. 20a), the worship of God through Christ is a natural corollary. . . . the immediate context in 2 Corinthians 1 . . . points rather to worship in general than prayer in particular as the background of the present usage. . . . the asserative particle *amēn* is the church's liturgical response to God . . . it points to their worshipful acknowledgment of the fulfillment of God's promises in the person and work of Christ" (Harris, *Corinthians*, 203-4).

audience to join him in this act of epistolary worship that thanks God for this "grace" that God is giving to Paul, the Corinthians, and all of "us" believers.[9]

Everything that the grace of God has accomplished in Paul's apostolic ministry is for the sake of his Corinthian audience. The result of this is that the "grace" (*charis*) that is bestowed on more and more people, including and especially the Corinthians, may cause the "thanksgiving" (*eucharistian*), the act of worship that gratefully acknowledges this "grace" that comes from God, to abound to the "glory" of God (4:15). In other words, Paul's apostolate aims to make the Corinthians participants in a widespread act of worship that increases in magnitude as it gratefully glorifies God for the magnificent grace that continues to be experienced by those who believe in the God who raised the Lord Jesus from the dead (4:14; cf. 1:11).[10]

If the Corinthians fail to be reconciled to God (5:20–6:2) and to Paul (6:3–13), Paul warns that they risk being linked with unbelievers (6:14–15). This would have negative repercussions for their status as "holy ones"—those who are separated from the world and consecrated to God (1:1). Indeed, as Paul reminds them, God has promised "I will dwell and walk among them, and I will be their God and they will be my people" (6:16b). As God's own people, "we are the temple of the living God" (6:16; cf. 1 Cor 3:16–17; 6:19). If the Corinthians separate themselves from unbelievers, God promises to welcome them (6:17), implying the acceptance of their worship as the holy temple of God. Since we have these promises, Paul urges his beloved Corinthian audience that "we cleanse ourselves of every defilement of flesh and spirit, making holiness complete in fear of God" (7:1). In other words, by reconciling themselves with God and Paul, the Corinthians will retain their status as God's holy temple capable of rendering acceptable worship in reverential fear of the living God.[11]

9. The objects of the triumphal procession are not captives but are incorporated into the triumphant Christ who is the parade, according to Hock ("Christ is the Parade," 110–19).

10. "Paul is envisaging that, with the expansion of God's grace by means of the conversion of an ever-growing multitude of people, the volume of thanksgiving to God for the receipt of illumination (cf. 4:6) would be greatly augmented and therefore God's greater glory would be achieved" (Harris, *Corinthians*, 357).

11. Adewuya, *Holiness and Community in 2 Cor. 6:14—7:1*; Goodwin, *Apostle of the Living God*, 190–207.

Worship in 2 Corinthians 8–9

Paul describes the collection of his churches for the holy ones in Jerusalem (cf. 1 Cor 16:1–3) in terms implying that it is an act of worship that gives thanks, praise, and glory to God. This collection of relief funds is characterized as a "grace" that is motivated by, participates in, and extends the grace of God, its ultimate source. The "grace of God" that has been given in the churches of Macedonia (8:1) is illustrated by their sincere and generous willingness to take part in the "grace" that is the collection in service of the holy ones (8:4). Paul encouraged Titus to complete for the Corinthians this "grace" (8:6), and wishes that his Corinthian audience may excel in this "grace" (8:7). This "grace" which is the collection is motivated by the "grace" of our Lord Jesus Christ, who, though being rich (divine), became poor (died), so that the Corinthians might become rich (participate in divine life) by this poverty (8:9).[12]

Paul then suddenly performs an epistolary act of worship as he exclaims "thanks," literally "grace," to God, who gave to Titus the same concern that Paul has for the Corinthians to complete the "grace" of this collection (8:16).[13] This thanksgiving or "grace to God" thus subtly serves to gratefully acknowledge and praise God as the ultimate source of the collection, repeatedly referred to as a "grace," freely given by the Pauline churches as a participation in and extension of the grace of God. This "grace" to be delivered by Paul and his coworkers to the church in Jerusalem is for the "glory" of the Lord himself (8:19), that is, its aim is an act of worship that gives glory to the Lord Jesus Christ and/ or the Lord God.[14]

Just as Paul applies the word "grace" to the collection to connote that it is freely and graciously given as a grace whose ultimate origin is God, and that it results in an act of worship that gives "thanks" or "grace" to God, so the word "blessing" (*eulogia*) used to refer to the collection connotes that it is generously given as a blessing ultimately from

12. On Paul's use of "grace" (*charis*) in 2 Cor 8–9, see Stegman, *Second Corinthians*, 192.

13. Ascough, "Background of 2 Cor 8.1–15," 584–99.

14. "One of Paul's motives—undoubtedly the dominant one—in prosecuting this relief fund was to enhance the glory of the Lord God, probably because the success of the project would prompt people to praise God (9:11–13)" (Harris, *Corinthians*, 604).

God that generates an act of worship that blesses or praises God. Paul considered it necessary to send some of his coworkers ahead of him to Corinth to arrange the collection beforehand, which he describes as the promised "blessing" of the Corinthians. In this way, the collection will be ready as a freely given "blessing" rather than as something forced upon them (9:5). Furthermore, as Paul explains, "one who sows sparingly will also reap sparingly, and one who sows on the basis of blessings will also reap on the basis of blessings" (9:6). In other words, if the Corinthians send the collection willingly and generously as a "blessing," it will be like sowing a bountiful seed from which they can expect to reap a rich harvest of bountiful "blessings" in return. It will inspire the recipients to acts of worship that not only bless God but also invoke God's abundant blessings upon the Corinthians.[15]

Reinforcing that God is the ultimate source of the collection as a "grace," Paul assures his audience that God is able to make every "grace" abundant for them (9:8). Indeed, the Corinthians are being enriched for every generosity, which is producing through Paul and his churches an act of worship, namely, "thanksgiving" (*eucharistian*) to God (9:11). But this involves not just a single act of worship. The service of this public ministry, which is the collection, is not only supplying the needs of the holy ones, but it is also overflowing through many "thanksgivings" to God (9:12). In fact, the proven character that this service indicates will prompt its recipients to the performance of doxological worship, as they will be "glorifying" God on the basis of the obedience of the confession of the Corinthians to the gospel of Christ and on the basis of the generosity of their sharing toward them and toward all (9:13).

---

15. "Words and ritual acts associated with 'blessing' are the primary means by which divine favor is invoked, distributed, acknowledged, and lauded in biblical and kindred Israelite, Jewish, and Christian traditions. . . . biblical sources insist that 'all blessings flow' from a single sublime source, 'God' the creator. . . . God's benefactions, together with human petitions for them, and ardent praise of God for blessings received are reciprocal actions in the biblical economy of divine providence" (McBride, "Bless," 476). According to Harris (*Corinthians*, 628), the collection "would be a blessing to the destitute believers in Jerusalem (9:12), that would prompt the Jerusalemites to bless God (9:11–13), and that would lead to God's gracious blessing on their own lives (9:8–10). On a broader plane, Paul saw the collection as a Gentile *eulogia* directed toward the Jerusalem church, a material 'blessing' given in gratitude for spiritual blessings."

The gracious and generous collection of the Corinthians will arouse the holy ones in Jerusalem not only to a widespread worship of glorifying God, but to the worship that consists of their prayers to God for the Corinthians. In acknowledgement that the generous "grace" of this collection has its origin in God, the holy ones in Jerusalem, in their "prayer" (*deēsei*) on behalf of the Corinthians, are longing for them on account of the surpassing "grace" of God upon them (9:14). The Paul who previously appealed for the "prayer" to God from the Corinthians on his behalf (1:11) now assures the Corinthians that the abundant divine grace evident in their generous collection will result in the benefit of the prayer to God from the holy ones in Jerusalem on their behalf.

Paul climaxes his exhortation regarding the collection with a stirring act of worship—"Thanks," literally "grace" (*charis*), "to God for his indescribable gift!" (9:15; cf. 2:24; 8:16). That this "gift" (*dōrea*) of God, with its connotations of a graciously and generously given bounty, is "indescribable" not only reinforces how the "grace" of God is surpassing or extraordinarily abundant (9:14), but seems to sum up all of the various and rich dimensions of the "grace" involved with this collection. This "indescribable gift" of God thus embraces the "grace of God" evident in the "grace" of our Lord Jesus Christ, who became poor that we might become rich, as the motivation for generous giving (8:6); the "grace" that is the collection, whose source is the grace of God (8:1, 4, 7, 19; 9:8, 14); the collection as the "blessing" from God that generates the giving of bountiful "blessings" in return (9:5–6); and the prayers that will be given by the holy ones in Jerusalem for the benefit of the Corinthians (9:14). With this exuberant exclamation Paul is thus leading his audience in an act of worship that thanks, acknowledges, and praises God for the inexhaustible abundance of all that he freely and generously gives as "grace."[16]

---

16. Joubert, "Religious Reciprocity in 2 Corinthians 9:6–15," 79–90. "With this concluding thanksgiving, therefore, Paul again emphasizes the relationship of the collection to God's overall work of redemption. To the extent that the generosity of the Macedonians and the Corinthians is an expression of God's grace, it reflects the work of God's salvation—the indescribable gift—in their lives" (Matera, *II Corinthians*, 210). "Having spoken of praising God for generous giving between humans, Paul now says in effect, 'Let us all give thanks to God for *his* supremely generous gift to us!'" (Harris, *Corinthians*, 659).

Worship in 2 Corinthians 10–13

In explaining how his authentic apostleship differs from that of the false, "super" apostles (11:13), Paul resorts to an ironical and paradoxical boasting about himself, as he declares, "If it is necessary to boast, I will boast about the things regarding my weakness" (11:30). He then employs a traditional oath formula invoking the omniscience of God, in which he inserts a traditional formula of worship, to guarantee his truthfulness in this matter, as he asserts, "The God and Father of the Lord Jesus knows, who is blessed forever, that I am not lying" (11:31; cf. 11:11; 12:2–3). Paul's traditional liturgical benediction here of God as the one who is "blessed" (*eulogētos*) forever (cf. Rom 1:25; 9:5) strengthens this solemn invocation as a divine attestation of his veracity, as it reminds his audience of how he led them in the letter's introductory benediction—"Blessed the God and Father of our Lord Jesus Christ" (1:3). In other words, the God Paul appeals to regarding his personal truthfulness is the same God both Paul and the Corinthians revere and respect in their communal worship. Furthermore, Paul's invocation of God and sudden exclamation of worship accords well with the overall worshiping context intended for his letter, as underscored by his insistence that he is speaking to the Corinthians in the presence of God in Christ (2:17; 12:19), as they are gathered for worship in God's presence.

Included in the weakness of which Paul paradoxically boasts (11:30) is what he describes as a rather mystifying "thorn in the flesh, an angel of Satan" to torment him lest he exalt himself (12:7).[17] Paul then provides his audience with an account of his own worship, his personal prayer report, regarding this matter. After he repeatedly—no less than three times—had implored the Lord that this would depart from him (12:8), he received the Lord's answer to his ardent prayer: "My grace is sufficient for you, for power is made perfect in weakness" (12:9a).[18] The answer Paul received through such praying enabled him to boldly declare that he will boast most gladly about his weaknesses, so that the power of Christ may dwell upon him (12:9b). Indeed, he is content with weaknesses, with insults, with troubles, with persecutions and difficul-

17. Abernathy, "Paul's Thorn in the Flesh" 69–79.

18. According to Harris (*Corinthians*, 859), the word used here for Paul's ardent prayer, *parakaleō*, in secular Greek "is a common word for invoking a deity for aid. In the Gospels it is regularly used to describe requests made to Jesus for his help."

ties for the sake of Christ, for "whenever I am weak, then I am strong" (12:10). This very personal and passionate prayer report provides Paul's audience with a model for how their own personal prayers to the God and Father of our Lord Jesus Christ as the source of divine grace and peace (1:2) can likewise enable them to experience the power of Christ in the midst of all of their weaknesses and difficulties.

As Paul begins the closing exhortation of the letter, he urges the Corinthians to test themselves to see if they are in the faith (13:5). He then performs another act of epistolary worship in the form of an intercessory prayer for his audience: "But we pray to God that you may not do anything wrong, not so that we may appear to have passed the test, but so that you may do what is right, even though we may seem to have failed the test" (13:7). This prayer is subsequently reinforced and clarified, as Paul emphasizes, "and for this we pray, your restoration" (13:9).[19] The first-person plural, "we pray" (*euchometha*), here refers primarily to Paul, but it does not have an entirely exclusive sense. To be sure, Paul uses the first-person plural for himself frequently throughout the letter, but for himself in relation to his audience as part of his rhetorical strategy. It subtly suggests that Paul and the Corinthians are involved together—he with them, and they with him—in the problems addressed in the letter. Solving them is their joint and mutual endeavor. Consequently, Paul's "we pray" poignantly hints that his Corinthian audience are to join him in this prayer.[20] Just as when Paul prayed for himself (12:8), when the Corinthians join him in praying for them-

19. "The Corinthians would be doing wrong or following the wrong path if they refused to repent of sin (cf. 6:14–7:1; 12:20–21; 13:2), if they continued to harbor Paul's rivals and their false gospel, or if they refused to recognize Paul as being *dokimos*, God's approved apostle to Corinth (cf. 10:13–14). On the other hand, they would be doing what was right or pursuing the right course if they once more (cf. 7:9) repented of wrongdoing, if they rejected the interlopers from Palestine, and if they fully embraced Paul and his gospel" (Harris, *Corinthians*, 924). And with regard to "your restoration," Harris (ibid., 928) explains, "The Corinthians needed to be restored to undivided and pure devotion to Christ (cf. 11:3), to uninhibited love for Paul (6:12–13; 12:15), and to harmonious fellowship with one another (cf. 12:20; 13:11)."

20. According to Wiles (*Paul's Intercessory Prayers*, 247), with his intercessory prayer here for the Corinthians Paul is "tacitly suggesting to a divided congregation that unitedly they join in his prayers for themselves."

selves, they, like him, can expect to experience the divine answer that "my grace is sufficient for you" (12:9).[21]

Before his own closing greeting, Paul directs his audience to greet one another with a "holy kiss," and assures them of a greeting from all the "holy ones," thus reminding them that they are in union with and enjoy the moral support of all of their fellow believers (13:12; cf. 1:1). Such a ritual "holy kiss" was especially appropriate among those who have been made "holy ones" by God. Its performance after the reading of the letter in the liturgical assembly would be a public demonstration of the communal unity, love, fellowship, and reconciliation Paul intends the letter to achieve.[22]

Paul closes the letter with his own personal greeting, a final reminder of key themes heard in the letter: "The grace of the Lord Jesus Christ and the love of God and the fellowship of the Holy Spirit with all of you" (13:13). Together with the opening greeting of the letter (1:2), this final greeting forms a literary inclusion that encloses the entire letter within a framework of worship. Like the letter's opening greeting this final greeting is verbless, which allows it to be heard as embracing a comprehensive temporal dimension. It affirms that "all" of the Corinthians have already, when they became believers, experienced grace, love, and fellowship as divine gifts that united them into a community of holy ones (1:1). It succinctly summarizes the divine gifts the Corinthian assembly are now experiencing anew as they listen

21. "The (intercessory) prayer of Paul here is thus an appeal to God for help and preservation. It is thus an expression of the weakness of believers who have their strength in Christ: to that extent it also has the character of an admonition to the Church" (Balz, "*euchomai*," 89).

22. "References to a 'holy kiss' occur at the conclusion of other Pauline letters (Rom 16:16; 1 Cor 16:20; 1 Thess 5:26), as well as in 1 Pet 5:14. Although the kiss eventually became a liturgical action and remains such today, it is difficult to determine if it had a role in the worship of the Pauline churches. Since this letter would have been read to an assembly of believers at Corinth, however, it is likely that Paul intended the Corinthians to exchange a holy kiss immediately after hearing his letter, whether or not the letter was read in the context of a liturgical setting. In calling upon the Corinthians to exchange a holy kiss, Paul is reinforcing his exhortation to reconciliation, since the holy kiss was undoubtedly an expression of peace and reconciliation among those who exchanged it. The gesture is described as a 'holy kiss' because those who exchanged it belonged to the assembly of 'the holy ones,' whom God had reconciled to himself through Christ" (Matera, *II Corinthians*, 313). "This type of kiss—that is, one that could cultivate spiritual union between two persons—may be what Paul intends in his common command to early Christian communities" (Powery, "Kiss," 536).

to the letter. And it functions as Paul's final epistolary act of worship in this letter, as he prays that his audience will continue to experience these divine gifts as they "all" together implement what the letter expects of them for the restoration of peace and reconciliation within the community.[23]

Conclusion: Worship in 2 Corinthians

To sum up, after Paul initiates the ritualistic worship of this letter in its opening greeting in which Paul prays for "grace to you and peace from God our Father and the Lord Jesus Christ" (1:2), he leads his Corinthian congregation in a communal act of worship that praises God with a liturgical benediction, "Blessed the God and Father of our Lord Jesus Christ, the Father of mercies and the God of all encouragement" (1:3). If the Corinthians join together in helping with prayer on behalf of Paul, then the divine gift of rescue from additional dangers to him in the province of Asia (1:10) that will be given to Paul through many prayers will result in a widespread worship of many persons giving thanks to God on behalf of Paul (1:11). Jesus Christ, in whom is the faithful and reliable "yes" to God's promises, not only motivates but mediates the worship of believers, as it is "through" Christ that the liturgical "amen" acknowledging and confirming the faithfulness of God in the worship that gives glory to God goes "through" us (1:20).

Paul then invites his audience to join him in an act of epistolary worship that thanks God for the "grace" of leading "us" believers in tri-

---

23. "This closing formula in 2 Corinthians is distinguished from all other Pauline grace benedictions by virtue of its two additional wishes ('love' and 'fellowship') and their two corresponding divine sources ('of God' and 'of the Holy Spirit'). These supplementary wishes of 'love' and 'fellowship' fit the thrust of the entire letter closing of 2 Corinthians, and, in turn, echo the concern of the entire letter—namely, that peace and harmony must exist within the Corinthian church" (Weima, *Neglected Endings*, 213). "Paul's tripartite formula focuses on the economy as effected by Christ, God, and the Spirit and as experienced by believers. Believers first experience the graciousness of Jesus Christ who died for all (5:11–12). On the basis of this gracious act, they come to know the love of God, who in Christ 'was reconciling the world to himself' (5:19). Having been reconciled by God's love, believers are given 'the first installment of the Spirit' (1:22) who establishes fellowship and communion among those who belong to the new covenant community. Paul's three-part blessing, therefore, prays for and reminds the Corinthians of the blessings of the economy of salvation" (Matera, *II Corinthians*, 314).

umph in Christ (2:14). Paul's apostolate aims to make the Corinthians participants in a widespread act of worship that increases in magnitude as it glorifies God for the grace that continues to be experienced by those who believe (4:14). By reconciling themselves with God and Paul (5:20–6:13), the Corinthians, as "holy ones," will retain their status as God's holy temple capable of rendering acceptable worship in reverential fear of the living God (6:16–7:1).

Paul describes the collection of his churches for the holy ones in Jerusalem (2 Corinthians 8–9) in terms implying that it is an act of worship that gives thanks, praise, glory, and blessing to God. His thanksgiving or "grace to God" (8:16) gratefully acknowledges and praises God as the ultimate source of the collection, repeatedly referred to as a "grace" (8:1, 4, 6, 7, 19), freely given by the Pauline churches as a participation in and extension of the grace of God. This "grace" to be delivered by Paul and his coworkers to the church in Jerusalem is for the "glory" of the Lord himself (8:19), that is, its aim is an act of worship that gives glory to the Lord Jesus Christ and/or the Lord God.

If the Corinthians send the collection willingly and generously as a "blessing," it will be like sowing a bountiful seed from which they can expect to reap a rich harvest of bountiful "blessings" in return, as it will inspire the recipients to acts of worship that not only bless God but invoke God's abundant blessings upon the Corinthians (9:5–6). The collection will prompt its recipients to the performance of doxological worship, as they will be "glorifying" God for the generosity of the Corinthians (9:11–13). The Paul who previously appealed for the "prayer" to God from the Corinthians on his behalf (1:11) assures the Corinthians that the divine grace evident in their generous collection will result in the benefit of the prayer to God from the holy ones in Jerusalem on their behalf (9:14). With an exuberant exclamation, "thanks/grace to God for his indescribable gift!" (9:15), Paul leads his audience in an act of worship that thanks, acknowledges, and praises God not only for the "grace" involved in the collection but for the inexhaustible abundance of all that he freely and generously gives as "grace."

The God Paul "blesses" in his appeal regarding his personal truthfulness (11:31) is the same God both Paul and the Corinthians "bless" in their communal worship (1:3). Paul's very personal and passionate prayer report (12:7–10) in which he received the divine answer that "my grace is sufficient for you, for power is made perfect in weakness" (12:9) provides his audience with a model for how their own personal prayers can likewise enable them to experience the power of Christ in the midst of all of their weaknesses and difficulties. When Paul twice declares that "we pray" to express his personal prayer on behalf of his Corinthian audience (13:7, 9), he is subtly but poignantly inviting them to join him and pray for themselves to experience, as did he, that "my grace is sufficient for you" (12:9). The performance of the ritual "holy kiss" (13:12) by the Corinthian "holy ones" after the reading of the letter in the liturgical assembly would be a public demonstration of the communal unity, love, fellowship, and reconciliation Paul intends the letter to achieve.

Finally, Paul's closing greeting, together with the opening greeting (1:2), encloses the entire letter within a framework of worship. Paul prays that "all" within his Corinthian audience, as a restored and united community, may continue to experience the divine gifts of grace, love, and fellowship, which they began to experience when they became believers and which listening to the letter has renewed for them: "The grace of the Lord Jesus Christ and the love of God and the fellowship of the Holy Spirit (was/is/will be) with all of you" (13:13).

Galatians

This letter is addressed to "the churches in Galatia" (Gal 1:2). There are two differing interpretations as to which area of Western Asia (modern Turkey) is being referred to here as "Galatia." One theory holds that it refers to northern Galatia, which included such cities as Ancyra, Tavium, and Pessinus, the old territory of the ethnic Galatians, descendants of the Celts. A second maintains that it refers rather to the Roman province in southern Galatia. According to this hypothesis, Paul was writing to the churches of Antioch in Pisidia, Lystra, Iconium, and Derbe, which he founded on his first missionary journey (Acts 13–14). Paul does not disclose the location from which he is sending the letter, but he includes "all the brothers who are with me" as senders of the letter (1:2).

It was because of some physical illness, literally "a weakness of the flesh," that Paul first proclaimed the gospel to the churches in Galatia. Although Paul's weak condition was a trial for the Galatians, they did not despise or disdain him. On the contrary, they welcomed him as "an angel of God, as Christ Jesus" (4:13–14). Since they were Gentiles, Paul did not require them to undergo the Jewish initiation rite of circumcision. They thus did not have to observe the "works of the law" such as dietary prescriptions and Sabbath observance. In other words, they did not have to engage in all of the practices of Jewish worship.

After Paul left Galatia, some Jewish Christian missionaries came and preached a "different gospel" (1:6), which called for the Galatians to have themselves circumcised and to observe the "works of the law." Although Paul did not require Jewish believers to renounce their Jewish heritage, according to the gospel he preached, it was not necessary for Gentile believers to adopt Jewish customs and practices of worship in order to be "justified," that is, brought into a right relationship with God. Paul thus wrote this very passionate letter to strongly urge the Galatians not to undergo circumcision and adopt the practices of Jewish worship.[1]

Galatians as a Ritual of Worship

Introductory Worship

Paul initiates the epistolary worship with a ritualistic greeting to the "churches" or "assemblies" (*ekklēsiais*) gathered, probably in various houses, to listen to the letter within a context of liturgical worship (1:2), as he pronounces, "grace to you and peace from God our Father and the Lord Jesus Christ" (1:3).[2] That Paul addresses the Galatians as "an apostle not from human beings nor through a human being but through Jesus Christ and God the Father who raised him from the dead" (1:1) establishes his divine authority to utter this pronouncement. As one sent to them through Jesus Christ and God the Father, Paul quite appropriately reminds his audience of the grace and peace that they, as believers, have already received from God the Father and the Lord Jesus Christ. Indeed, the implication is that his being sent to them as a divinely authorized apostle is part of that grace. His greeting also indicates that the letter intends, and possesses the power, to effectively communicate to them a renewed experience of this grace and peace. And it functions as Paul's prayer that after and as a result of listening to the letter as a liturgical assembly they will continue to experience the divine gifts of grace and peace.

The divine gift of this "grace" is further described as coming from the Lord Jesus Christ, who "gave" himself for our sins that he might deliver us out of this present evil age according to the will of our God and Father (1:4). Paul then leads his audience in an act of doxological worship in response to this marvelous divine gift, as he exclaims, "to whom the glory for the ages of the ages. Amen!" (1:5). This exuberant doxology acknowledges and praises God for the magnificent "glory" (*doxa*) that

1. Matera, "Galatians," 476–77; idem, *New Testament Theology*, 152–53. See also Soards, "Galatians," 508–14.

2. Suggit, "Galatians 1:3," 97–103.

has always been, still is, and always will be his distinguished characteristic forever and ever. Paul potently punctuates this sudden burst of worship with the solemn liturgical formula of affirmation and assent intended to reverberate throughout the worshiping assembly—"Amen!"[3]

Paul expresses his great astonishment that the Galatians are so quickly turning away from the God who called them by the "grace" of Christ and following a gospel different from the one Paul preached to them (1:6). Such an abandonment of the God who calls them by "grace" contradicts the doxological worship of God in response to that "grace," the worship in which Paul has just engaged them (1:5). That God also called Paul through his "grace" to preach the gospel to the Gentiles (1:15) further confirms how Paul's apostleship and gospel are part of the "grace" that motivates worship.[4] Rather than contradicting their doxological worship inspired by the "grace" of God, the churches in Galatia should be following the example of the churches of Judea that are in Christ (1:22). When they heard that Paul was now proclaiming the gospel of the faith he once tried to destroy (1:23), they were motivated by the "grace" manifested in Paul (cf. 2:9) to offer doxological worship. They "glorified" (*edoxazon*) God on account of Paul (1:24).[5]

---

3. "The 'glory' of the God of Israel in the OT is primarily the radiance of his presence; when 'glory' is ascribed to him it denotes the transcendent praise and worship of which he is worthy. . . . As this letter was read in the churches of Galatia, the hearers would add their 'Amen' to Paul's at the end of the doxology, thus endorsing the ascription of glory to God (cf. 2 Cor 1:20)" (Bruce, *Galatians*, 77–78). "In v 4 Paul probably draws on an early Christian *confession*. He then pronounces a solemn *doxology* (v 5), and he closes the sentence with the word *amēn*, an exclamation by which worshipers are invited to participate in a blessing, a prayer, or a doxology. Taken as a whole, then, vv 3–5 do not merely extend Paul's greetings. They have the effect of evoking the setting of worship. . . .We may assume that Paul brings the doxology from its usual liturgical setting into this epistolary introduction in order to make clear that the reading of this letter belongs properly to the context of worship" (Martyn, *Galatians*, 87, 91, emphases original). See also Van Voorst, "Why Is There No Thanksgiving Period in Galatians?" 171.

4. "Probably Paul has in mind God here as ultimately the one who called them in grace, though Paul was the agent of God in this" (Witherington, *Grace in Galatia*, 82).

5. "'[T]hey glorified God on my account'—every time they heard such news (imperfect tense)—because of the transforming grace that had been manifested 'in me'" (Bruce, *Galatians*, 105).

Meal Fellowship and Worship

The gospel that Paul preached had ramifications for the worship that took place in and through the meals shared by believers, which possessed a sacred character and included the eucharistic celebration of the Lord's Supper.[6] Paul reports to the Galatians an incident that took place in Antioch involving Peter and the corporate worship that took place within the meals shared by both Jewish and Gentile believers. Until certain people came to Antioch from James in Jerusalem, Peter used to "eat with," that is, share meal fellowship with, the Gentile believers. But when these people, who advocated that Gentiles must be circumcised and thus become Jewish, arrived, Peter began to draw back and "separated" (*aphorizen*) himself—a technical cultic term—from this kind of worship (2:12). The rest of the Jews, including Barnabas, followed Peter in this cultic "separation" of themselves from the meal fellowship of "eating with," and thus worshiping with, Gentiles (2:13).[7]

But when Paul saw that they were not behaving correctly with regard to the truth of the gospel, he chastised Peter in front of all, "If you, being a Jew, are living like a Gentile and not like a Jew, how can you force the Gentiles to live like Jews?" (2:14). Paul goes on to explain that even Jews are "justified" and thus brought into a right relationship to

---

6. "In sum, the Christian sacred meals reflected in the NT and other very early Christian texts likely were varied in what was done and in what they meant for the participants. But in all cases, Jesus was the central figure for whom and with whom thanks were offered to God, and the meal itself was a central feature of Christian corporate worship across various circles of the Christian movement. Further, as a group meal, there was an emphasis on the solidarity of those who partook; it was a corporate action and not that of individuals in some private act of devotion" (Hurtado, "Worship," 922–23).

7. According to Kellermann ("*aphorizō*," 184), "*aphorizō* became a technical term for the dissolution of cultic community (Gal 2:12). Peter *separated* himself *from* table fellowship between Gentile and Jewish Christians and held the Lord's Supper for the Jewish Christians separately when the 'visitors' from James arrived." "The Jerusalem church, truly observant of the Law, held its common meals—including the Eucharist—in accordance with the Jewish food laws. . . . In the Antioch church, however, the meals—again including the Eucharist—were arranged by an adjustment on the part of the members who were Jews by birth. At least by implication, the food laws were declared to be essentially a matter of no consequence in the church. . . . Since the Eucharist was part of the common meal, Peter's withdrawal from the latter brought with it his withdrawal from the former. He has now separated himself from the Gentile members, as they eat the Lord's Supper" (Martyn, *Galatians*, 232–33).

God, so that they may properly worship God, not from the works of the Jewish law but through faith in Christ (2:15–16). The implication for the Galatians is that they do not need to have themselves circumcised and become Jewish in order to be able to worship God properly, including the worship that takes place in and through their meals.[8]

Baptism and Ethical Worship

As Paul points out, it was not through Jewish circumcision but through faith in Christ Jesus that all of the Galatians are "sons" of God (3:26). Faith in Christ Jesus was sacramentally ritualized in a ceremonial immersion with water known as "baptism," an initiation rite that replaced the Jewish initiation rite of circumcision.[9] The Galatians who were baptized into Christ have "clothed themselves" with Christ (3:27). The metaphor of "clothing oneself" was a symbol of the transformation of one's very life and way of living. This spiritual "clothing" of oneself with Christ in baptism thus initiated a new behavior and conduct in accord with Christ that was part of ethical or moral worship. This is further indicated as Paul goes on to proclaim, "There is neither Jew nor Greek, there is neither free nor slave, there is neither male nor female, for all of you are one in Christ Jesus" (3:28). Having been "clothed" with Christ in baptism thus means that there is no longer a need for Jewish and Gentile believers to worship separately. All believers are now members of one and the same community who live for and worship God in Christ Jesus both liturgically and ethically.[10]

---

8. "This reference indicates that the practice of circumcision includes more than simply performing the physical act itself. Practicing circumcision also means maintaining distinctions between the circumcised and the uncircumcised (Gen 17:14), especially by refusing to engage in table fellowship" (Martin, "Circumcision in Galatia," 228).

9. "Thus Christian water-and-Spirit baptism replaces the mark of Jewish circumcision" (Taylor, "Baptism," 394).

10. "Clothing's function as an object of societal symbolism allows it to serve as a symbol of life itself. Garments indicate gender, membership in a community or profession, and as a metaphor encompassing both proper and improper behavior" (Matthews, "Clothe Oneself," 696). "For Paul, the very composition of the people of God that includes both Jews and Gentiles denies circumcision as a requirement for holiness" (Martin, "Circumcision," 231).

That being "clothed" with Christ in baptism indicates a transformation to a new way of living and worshiping (3:27) recalls and resonates with Paul's previous proclamation of this new and total transformation of life. Employing the first-person singular to refer not only to himself personally but to speak as the preeminent representative of every believer, Paul explains, "For I through the law died, so that I might live for God. I have been crucified with Christ, and I live—no longer I, but Christ lives in me, and insofar as I now live in the flesh, I live by faith in the Son of God who loved me and gave himself up for me" (2:19–20). Christ's love and sacrificial "giving himself up" not only for Paul but for every believer is a further expression of the "grace" of the Lord Jesus Christ, who "gave himself" for our sins (1:3–4). It was this divine grace that motivated the liturgical worship of Paul and the Galatians, expressed in their giving "glory" to God (1:5). And this divine grace now motivates the ethical worship of every believer who has been "clothed" with Christ in baptism, so as, like Paul, to "live for God." How it is this divine grace that now motivates this new way of living that worships God ethically is confirmed as Paul continues, "I do not reject the grace of God, for if righteousness is through law, then Christ died for nothing" (2:21).

Freedom for Worship in the Spirit

As "sons" of God (3:26) who have reached the age of being "heirs" (4:3), the Galatians are no longer "slaves" deprived of an inheritance, no longer "enslaved" to the elemental powers of the world that prevent them from properly worshiping God. Now that the fullness of time has arrived, God has sent his Son (4:4) to redeem those enslaved under the law, so that we believers might receive "sonship" (4:5) with full rights of inheritance. This includes inheriting the promise of God's own Spirit (3:14). Consequently, God has sent into the hearts of us who are "sons" of God the Spirit of his Son, who cries out within us as we are gathered as a community for liturgical worship, "Abba! Father!" (4:6; cf. Rom 8:15). We believers are thus privileged to be members of God's family and to address God as our own Father as we worship liturgically. But we also have the responsibility of offering ethical worship to God as our Father by the way we conduct our lives.[11]

Before they became believers, the Galatians did not know the true God. Since they were then enslaved to beings that by nature are not gods at all (4:8), they were not capable of worshiping the one and only true God. If they undergo the Jewish ritual of circumcision, they will be turning back again to these weak and worthless elements and become enslaved to them again (4:9). Indeed, as Paul draws to their attention, they are already engaged in Jewish practices of worship, as they are "carefully observing days and months and seasons and years" (4:10), which seem to be a reference to Jewish sabbaths, feasts, and other religious days.[12]

But the Spirit that God sent into the hearts of us believers frees us from slavery to what is opposed to God and empowers us not only to worship God liturgically by crying out, "Abba! Father!" (4:6), but to worship God ethically, not fulfilling the desire of the flesh, but "walking," that is, conducting our lives by the Spirit (5:16). If the Galatians allow their lives to be led and guided by the Spirit, they will not be enslaved to the realm of the flesh under the Jewish law (5:18). The fruits

---

11. "[E]ven though the *Abba*-cry is very much the realized experience of individual believers, the cry itself is most likely to be heard in the gathered worship of the community. . . . we need to take seriously that believers 'cried out' to God within the assembly, and did so with full awareness that the Spirit was moving them so to do, and that they were thus using Jesus' own word of intimate relationship with the Father" (Fee, *God's Empowering Presence*, 409–10). "[H]onour is ascribed to us because of our association with God as 'Father' and our belonging to his family. Indeed, this relationship also brings an accompanying moral responsibility for God's children to live in ways that bring glory to their adoptive Father and to his family name. The expression '*Abba*, Father' also enables adopted sons to address God in prayer through the Spirit; and in doing so they use the same language Jesus, God's Son, used in communion with the Father. *Abba* was a term that found its way into the Gentile-speaking churches of Paul because Jesus had taught his disciples to address God in this way. And because *Abba*'s sons are also *Abba*'s heirs, the inheritance believers can look forward to is God himself" (Burke, *Adopted into God's Family*, 99).

12. "The point of this verse is to draw a close parallel between what the Galatians used to do in regard to religious observances and what they are now doing or at least contemplating doing by following the Mosaic Law. Without question, the agitators would never have agreed that following the Mosaic Law was anything like practicing pagan rituals or participating in the worship of the Emperor, but that is what Paul's analogy is meant to suggest, in so far as the effect on the worshipper is concerned" (Witherington, *Grace in Galatia*, 301–2).

of the Spirit, in contrast to the works of the flesh (5:19–21), describe the ethical worship empowered by the Spirit and demonstrated by behavior such as "love, joy, peace, patience, kindness, generosity, faithfulness, gentleness, self-control" (5:22–23). If the Galatians bear one another's burdens through love, they will thus fulfill the "law of Christ" (6:2), epitomized by the commandment that "you shall love your neighbor as yourself" (Lev 19:18), which fulfills the whole law (5:14).[13] If one "sows to the flesh," he will "reap corruption from the flesh," but if one "sows to the Spirit," which includes the practice of loving one's neighbor as oneself, he will "reap eternal life from the Spirit" (6:8). God is thereby not "mocked" (6:7) by such behavior, on the contrary such behavior renders appropriate and proper worship to God.[14]

Worship in the Letter's Closing

As he begins to bring the letter to a close, Paul pronounces a prayer for all those who will follow the rule that he has put forth in the letter, which includes especially that the Galatians not undergo the Jewish ritual of circumcision. He prays that the divine gifts of peace (cf. 5:22) and mercy will be upon them.[15] That he further identifies "upon them" as "upon the Israel of God" (6:16) provides his Galatian audience with an explicit and emphatic assurance that they are members of the chosen people of God, the "Israel of God," as believing members of the "church of God" (1:13) without becoming Jewish by having themselves circumcised.[16]

13. "The 'law of Christ' is not essentially different from the commandment of love to one's neighbor, in which 'the whole law' is comprehended" (Bruce, *Galatians*, 261).

14. "Paul awakens those into whose hearts God has already sent the Spirit (4:6), reminding them both of the Flesh's genuine power and of the Spirit's ultimate power" (Martyn, *Galatians*, 553).

15. "The apostle concludes this paragraph of brief reiterations of the chief ideas of the letter with a benediction upon all whose life is conformed to the great principle for which he has been contending, viz., the essentially spiritual character of religion as against the ascription of fundamental religious value to any physical or material condition, however sanctioned" (Burton, *Galatians*, 357).

16. For the interpretation of the Israel of God as the church of God, see Martyn, *Galatians*, 574–77; Witherington, *Grace in Galatia*, 451–53; "If one takes the context of the letter seriously, it seems much better to conclude that the phrase 'the Israel of God' refers to those Gentile Christians in Galatia who walk according to Paul's rule" (Weima, *Neglected Endings*, 97).

When Paul goes on to request that from now on let no one cause him troubles, the implication is that no one should oppose him regarding his insistence that believing Gentiles need not become Jewish by undergoing the rite of circumcision. For, as he explains, "I bear the marks of Jesus on my body" (6:17). More important than the physical mark that circumcision leaves on the body are the "marks" (*stigmata*) of Jesus that Paul bears on his body. In addition to referring to the physical scars Paul incurred on his body through his apostolic labors (cf. 2 Cor 4:10–11; Acts 14:19), the "marks" of Jesus on Paul's body carry a worship connotation. There was a practice in antiquity of tattooing marks on one's body to indicate religious devotion to a divinity. That Paul bears the "marks of Jesus" on his body suggests that the various scars and wounds he has received in the course of his ministry for the gospel are part of his ethical worship of God. These "marks of Jesus" thus resonate with and reinforce Paul's previous pronouncement that, rather than rejecting the grace of God (2:21), he responds to it by offering worship to God. He has been crucified with Christ that he might live for God (2:19). Paul worships God not with the mark of Jewish circumcision but with the "marks of Jesus" on his body.[17]

This final prayer that the grace of the Lord Jesus Christ, which has been and still is with them, will continue to be with "your spirit, brothers" (6:18), provides the Galatian audience with a final reminder of how their human "spirit" has been transformed by the divine "Spirit" of God's Son, which they have received as a grace from God. This Spirit has empowered them to offer proper worship to God not by undergoing the Jewish ritual of circumcision but by their faith in Christ. This prayer that the divine grace of the Lord Jesus Christ be with the human "spirit" of the Galatians, addressed as "brothers" by Paul and all the "brothers" with him (1:2), climaxes all of the letter's previous references to their reception of the divine Spirit that made them sons of God (4:6) and brothers of one another within the worshiping household of God.

---

17. BDAG, 945; "In contrast to the now irrelevant mark of circumcision, Paul asserts that he has marks on his body which do mean something real—the *stigmata* or scars which he has acquired as the direct consequence of his service for Jesus. These proclaim whose he is and whom he serves. . . . It has been pointed out that the term *stigmata* was used of the tattoo-marks by which devotees of various religious cults were identified as worshippers of this or that divinity" (Bruce, *Galatians*, 276).

Paul reminded them that they received the Spirit from faith not from works of the Jewish law (3:2, 5, 14). After beginning with the Spirit, they will be ending with the flesh, if they have themselves circumcised (3:5). God sent the Spirit of his Son into their hearts, enabling them to cry out in their liturgical worship, "Abba! Father!" (4:6). Just as the one born according to the flesh (Ishmael) persecuted the one born according to the Spirit (Isaac), so now those insisting upon Jewish circumcision are persecuting the Galatians (4:29). It is through the Spirit, from faith, that we await the hope of righteousness (5:5). The Galatians are to conduct their lives by the Spirit in order not to fulfill the desire of the flesh by being circumcised (5:16). Although the flesh desires against the Spirit, and the Spirit against the flesh, the Galatians are guided by the Spirit (5:17–18). They are able to offer ethical worship as a fruit of the Spirit (5:22–23). They who live by the Spirit should follow the lead of the Spirit (5:25). They who are Spiritual should correct one who has sinned with a Spirit of gentleness (6:1; cf. 5:23). And, finally, one who "sows" to the Spirit, from the Spirit will "reap" eternal life (6:8).[18] Paul concludes the letter with his prayer that the gift of this divine Spirit, as the preeminent grace of the Lord Jesus Christ, continues to be with the spirit of the Galatians (6:18), enabling them to offer proper worship to God.

In addition, Paul's verbless pronouncement of the letter's final greeting, "The grace of the Lord Jesus Christ with your spirit, brothers. Amen!" (6:18), completes a literary inclusion with the letter's initial act of worship. His prayer that the gift of "peace" that comes from God be upon the "Israel of God" (6:16) echoes the proclamation of "peace from God our Father" in the initial greeting (1:3). And his prayer that the grace of the Lord Jesus Christ that has been and still is with your spirit may continue to be with your spirit resonates with his prayer that the grace that has been and still is given to you from the Lord Jesus Christ may continue to be given to you (1:3). Furthermore, the solemn "Amen!" that concludes the letter invites the audience to add their final assenting confirmation to the epistolary worship. It reverberates with their "Amen!" that concluded the letter's initial worship (1:5). This literary inclusion formed by the letter's introductory (1:3–5) and con-

---

18. Fee, *God's Empowering Presence*, 377–471.

cluding acts of worship (6:16–18) thus places the entire letter within a context of prayerful worship.[19]

Conclusion: Worship in Galatians

In sum, rather than contradicting their doxological worship inspired by the "grace" of God (1:3–5), the churches in Galatia, like those of Judea (1:22), should offer the doxological worship of glorifying God on account of Paul (1:24) and his gospel that eliminates the need for believing Gentiles to undergo the Jewish initiation ritual of circumcision. Paul's chastisement of Peter for cultically "separating" himself from the worship, including the Eucharist, that took place within the meals shared by both Jews and Gentiles at Antioch (2:11–14) indicates that the Galatians do not need to have themselves circumcised and become Jewish in order to be able to worship God fully and properly. The "grace" of the Lord Jesus Christ, who "gave himself" for our sins (1:3–4), motivates the ethical worship of every believer who has been "clothed" with Christ in the ritual act of baptism, so as, like Paul, to "live for God" as a way of worshiping God ethically (2:19–20).

The Spirit that God sent into the hearts of us believers empowers us not only to worship God liturgically by crying out, "Abba! Father!" (4:6), but to worship God ethically by conducting our lives in accord with the fruits of the Spirit (5:16)—"love, joy, peace, patience, kindness, generosity, faithfulness, gentleness, self-control" (5:22–23). Paul concludes the letter with his prayer that the gift of the divine Spirit, as the preeminent grace of the Lord Jesus Christ, continues to be with the spirit of the Galatians (6:18), enabling them to offer proper worship to God. The literary inclusion formed by the letter's introductory (1:3–5) and concluding acts of worship (6:16–18), each of which evokes a resounding "Amen!" on the part of Paul's Galatian audience, places the entire letter within a context of prayerful worship and praise of God.

---

19. With regard to this final "Amen!," Bruce (*Galatians*, 277) remarks, "It would form the congregation's response to the reading of the letter; it would be pleasant to think that a well-meant and hearty 'Amen' was forthcoming in all the congregations to which this letter was sent." "The letter thus ends where it began, with the invocation of God and God's will" (Witherington, *Grace in Galatia*, 458).

Romans

Paul's letter to the Romans is arguably the most prominent of all his letters, often considered to contain the fullest theological exposition of the gospel Paul preached. When Paul dictated this letter to a scribe named Tertius (Rom 16:22), he was in all likelihood in the city of Corinth. Having fully completed the preaching of the gospel from Jerusalem to Illyricum (15:19), an area embracing the eastern Mediterranean regions, Paul stood at a crossroads in his apostolic ministry, no longer having room for the work of preaching the gospel in these regions (15:22). Consequently, he planned to travel to Jerusalem to deliver to the Jewish Christians there the monetary contribution collected by his Gentile churches in these regions, not only as a charitable gift for needy believers, but in respectful recognition of their status as the "mother" church and in hope of receiving their approval of his often controversial ministry to Gentiles.

After a hopefully favorable reception of this collection Paul planned to visit the Christian community in Rome, bringing with him "the fullness of the blessing of Christ" for them from Jerusalem (15:29). Although Paul had not founded a church at Rome, the lengthy list of those to be greeted at the conclusion of the letter indicates that several associates of Paul were now residing there. Paul hopes to see his Roman audience in passing on his way to Spain for apostolic work in the western Mediterranean regions, and to be sent on his way there by the Roman church, once he has enjoyed their company for a while (15:24, 28).[1]

As an apostle who preaches the gospel to the Gentiles, Paul longs to visit his fellow believers in Rome. Since the faith of his Roman audi-

---

1. Heil, *Paul's Letter to the Romans*, 162–75.

75

ence is world renowned (1:8), the spiritual strength and encouragement Paul wants to impart to them (1:11–12) describe the hope that is a consequence of this faith.[2] Before his arrival Paul will begin to spiritually strengthen and encourage his Roman audience with this hope as they listen to Paul communicating it to them in the letter itself, an epistolary medium and mode for his personal presence. In his letter to the Romans Paul thus activates for his audience the great hope that arises from their faith, a hope that finds a prominent expression in their worship, both the liturgical worship that takes place in their ecclesial assemblies and the ethical worship that takes place in their everyday lives. Let us now listen to Paul's great letter to the Romans as a ritual of worship.

Romans as a Ritual of Worship

Paul's Initial Worship in the Letter

Paul addresses the letter to all those in Rome, beloved of God and called as "holy ones" (1:7a), that is, as those who have been set apart by God and consecrated for the worship of God.[3] Paul's opening greeting to them, "grace to you and peace from God our Father and the Lord Jesus Christ" (1:7b), initiates the ritualistic worship of the letter and establishes a liturgical tone for it. This greeting contains no verb, which allows it to be heard at three levels of temporal aspect. First, it reminds the audience of the divine grace and peace they have already received in the past when they became believers. Second, it commences a renewed experience of that divine grace and peace in the present as they listen to the letter. And third, it prays that in the future they may continue to experience that divine grace and peace as a result of listening to Paul's letter.[4]

---

2. Heil, *Romans—Paul's Letter of Hope*, 12–13.

3. "In 1:7 the Roman Christians' calling makes them now holy people. The idea in the verse is not that holiness or sainthood is to be an ambition to be fulfilled. They already have this status and . . . Paul must see it as a decisive element of their identity" (Oakes, "Holiness and Ecclesiology in Romans," 175).

4. "It is important to grasp that for Paul, behind the whole salvation process always lay the initiative of God. No other word expresses his theology so clearly on this point as 'grace' (*charis*). For it summed up not only the epochal event of Christ itself but also the grace which made the vital breakthrough in individual human experience. And it

Paul then immediately performs an epistolary act of worship in response to that amazing grace. He proclaims, "First, I thank my God through Jesus Christ concerning all of you" (1:8). A wordplay indicates how this thanksgiving closely corresponds to God's grace. In Greek the word for "grace" is *charis*, while the word for "I thank" is *eucharistō*. One could paraphrase Paul's "I thank," then, as "I gratefully acknowledge, appreciate, and give praise" for the grace and peace that come from God our Father and the Lord Jesus Christ (1:7). Here Paul models for his Roman audience how the grace and peace available to them is to spark their worship of God through Jesus Christ as a response of respectful, reverent, and joyous gratitude.

Continuing to set the liturgical tone of the letter at its outset, Paul next declares, "For God is my witness, whom I worship (*latreuō*) with my spirit in the gospel of his Son, how ceaselessly I make mention of you always in my prayers, pleading that somehow, sometime, at last I may succeed by God's will to come to you" (1:9–10).[5] As those for whom Paul constantly prays, the Romans are to be impressed by how important they are to Paul and his apostolate and by how ardently he wishes to come to them. But here Paul also models for them how authentic petitionary prayer is ultimately a matter of acknowledging and subordinating oneself to the sovereign will of God.

Paul as Leader of Worship in the Letter

Paul gives further expression to the dynamic saving grace of God featured in the initial greeting that established the liturgical tone of the letter, when he describes his gospel as "the power of God for salvation

---

defined not only the past act of God initiating into a life of faith, but also present continuing experience of divine enabling" (Dunn, *Theology of Paul the Apostle*, 319–20). See also Lieu, "'Grace to You and Peace,'" 161–78.

5. The Greek verb here translated as "I worship" is often translated as "I serve." But it has the connotation of the service that is part of cultic worship (see BDAG, 587). "Since this verb is employed in the LXX predominantly in reference to cultic service, it places Paul's missionary prayers within the context of 'religious service' performed as 'worship' of God. This liturgical view of Paul's missionary activity recurs in 15:16, placing the entire project of the Spanish mission within the context of the worship that all believers owe to God" (Jewett, *Romans*, 120). See also Matera, *Romans*, 32.

to all who believe, to Jew first but also to Greek" (1:16).[6] He immediately begins spiritually to strengthen and encourage his Roman audience with the hope that springs from their faith as he goes on to assert that the righteousness of God is revealed in the gospel from faith to faith, and, according to the prophetic writing in Hab 2:4, "the one who is righteous from faith will live" (1:17). In other words, one who has accepted within the realm of faith the righteousness of God—that is the gracious gift ("the grace") from God—acquires the hope for an eternal life that begins with how one lives presently.

Since the "righteousness of God" is now revealed in the gospel, the corresponding obverse, the judgmental "wrath of God," is also now revealed from heaven upon all ungodliness and unrighteousness of those who suppress the truth by unrighteousness (1:18). False worship stands out as a key feature of this ungodliness. According to Paul, the ungodly in the Roman world exchanged the truth about God for a lie and reverenced and worshiped the creature instead of the Creator. But with a sudden and stunning interjection at precisely this point, Paul leads the audience into a true and proper worship of God as the Creator by quickly exclaiming, "who is blessed forever! Amen!" (1:25). Paul thus draws his audience into this poignant act of ritualistic worship, as his reverent benediction—exuberantly reinforced by a liturgically resounding "Amen!"—is intended to generate his fellow Roman believers' own reverberating benediction and reaffirming "Amen!"[7]

Paul goes on to insist that not only the ungodly but all, Jews as well as Greeks, are under the devastating power of sin (3:9). So pervading is this power that it deprives even their organs of speech of the ability to worship God, as indicated by a subsequent list of scriptural citations that confirm this scathing indictment: "Their *throat* is an opened grave; with their *tongues* they deceive [Ps 5:9]; the poison of asps is under their *lips* [Ps 140:3]; their *mouth* is filled with cursing and bitterness [Ps

---

6. Nolland, "Grace as Power," 26–31; Eastman, *Grace in the Letters of Paul*; Harrison, *Paul's Language of Grace*.

7. "To use the terminology of contemporary semantics, a biblical blessing is a performative utterance whose power resides not in the magical efficacy of the words themselves but in the authority of the speaker, the appropriateness of the situation, and the ultimate power of God to sustain the promised blessing. All three conditions pertain here, as Paul breaks into the mood of prayer that has both an illocutionary and a perlocutionary force; that is, the prayer thanks God for the concrete blessing of the creation and invites others to join the speaker in praising God" (Jewett, *Romans*, 171).

10:7]." In other words, instead of praising, blessing, or glorifying God with their throat, tongues, lips, and mouth (3:13–14, 19), the scriptural list concludes that "there is no reverence of God before their eyes [Ps 36:1]" (3:18).

But after Paul reaffirms that the righteousness of God has been manifested through faith in Jesus Christ for all who believe (3:21), he indicates how Abraham, the patriarch made righteous by God through faith (4:1–3), provides his Roman audience with a prime example of proper worship. On account of the promise of the God who gives life to the dead that Abraham would have numerous descendants despite his "deadened" old age, Abraham did not doubt in disbelief but was strengthened in faith, as he "gave glory to God" (4:20) in and through his hope (4:18). That Abraham gave glory to God is an act of worship, a doxology. "Giving glory" to God or "glorifying" God appropriately acknowledges that any glory human beings seek or possess comes from God (2:7, 10). In contrast to the false worship of the ungodly who exchanged the "glory" of the immortal God for an image of mortal man (1:23), and to all who are unable to worship because the power of sin has deprived them of the "glory" of God (3:23), Abraham "gave glory" to the God who gives life to the dead. He thus stands as a stellar model of worship for all who believe and have hope in the God who raised Jesus our Lord from the dead (4:24).[8]

Abraham believed in the God who gives life to the dead and thereby gave glory to God as a model of worship for Christians, who believe in the God who raised Jesus from the dead, to give glory to God by a new way of moral living as part of their ethical worship. A ritualistic act of worship, the sacrament of baptism, makes possible this ethical or moral worship of Christians. Paul pointedly informs his audience that when we were ritually baptized as Christians, we all sacramentally participated and shared in the actual death of Jesus Christ. We were "buried," that is, totally and definitively immersed, with him by our baptism into his death.[9] Since we were sacramentally joined with him

8. Neyrey, *Give God the Glory*, 139. See also Blackwell, "Romans 3.23," 285–308.

9. "Baptism in Romans 6 is a burial (v. 4) because—in line with the application of funerary rites elsewhere—it marks departure or separation from a previous situation or condition, or in Paul's language, the death of the old self (v. 6). From the standpoint of the Mediterranean ritual world, therefore, baptism according to Romans 6 was an imaginary funeral" (DeMaris, *Ritual World*, 64–65).

in his death, we may also now live a new life, a life that includes ethical worship, in correspondence to the risen life he now lives after having been raised from the dead by the powerful "glory" of God the Father (6:3–4). By this newness of life, this new ethical way of living, Christians may thus worship by giving glory to the God of glory.[10] Indeed, they may no longer yield the parts of their bodies to the power of sin, recalling how this devastating power prevented their throats, tongues, lips, and mouths from worshiping God (3:13–14, 18–19). Instead, they may yield themselves to God for the proper worship of God as those brought from death to life (6:13).[11]

Paul then further illustrates how the "grace" of God to which Christians have gained access by their faith (5:2) inspires a worship of God that acknowledges God precisely as the source of this powerful grace. Similar to Abraham who gave "glory" to the God who gives "glory," Paul attributes "grace" to the God who gives "grace." He leads his audience in this worship as he exclaims, "Grace to God (usually translated as "thanks to God," but the Greek word here is literally "grace"), that though you were slaves of sin you have become wholeheartedly obedient to the pattern of teaching to which you were committed" (6:17). A little later, with a profound prayer of lament, Paul expresses the utter despair of the individual trapped by the power of sin: "What a wretched person I am! Who will rescue me from this body of death?" (7:24). He immediately answers with an exuberant act of laudatory worship that again attributes grace to the God who gives grace: "Grace to God through Jesus Christ our Lord!" (7:25).[12]

Although, according to Paul, those who live in the flesh cannot please God (8:8), we believers, as those who have received the Spirit of sonship, are able to cry out in the liturgical assembly with an exclamation of an intimately filial worship, "Abba! Father!" (8:15). We are able to relate to, please, and worship God as God's very own children, who

---

10. "That believers are enabled through their burial in Christ's death to 'walk in newness of life' . . . places Paul and all of his hearers in the position of having already participated in this new ethic that displays the glory of God" (Jewett, *Romans*, 399–400).

11. "Rather than continuing to place themselves at the disposal of sin in its deadly human and institutional manifestations, believers are admonished to lend themselves to the service of God as persons 'made alive from the dead'" (ibid., 410).

12. Banks, "Romans 7:25a," 34–42.

have the hope of being glorified with Christ (8:16).[13] So tremendously transcendent is the future, invisible goal of this great hope that it is humanly impossible for us to pray for it as we ought. But Paul assures us that as we pray for it, the Spirit of God intercedes for us with wordless groanings to ensure that we pray in accord with the will of God (8:26–27).[14]

When he begins to address the problem of unbelieving Jews, Paul lists "worship" as one of their many privileges and prerogatives as God's chosen people (9:4). Paul, himself a Jew, then climaxes this list with his own act of worship that praises God for the Christ who came from the Jewish people. Since it was from the Jewish people that the Christ came according to the flesh, Paul exclaims, "God who is over all is blessed forever! Amen!" (9:5). Whereas previously Paul led his audience in an exuberant act of the true worship of God as Creator with this same ritualistic benediction and amen (1:25), here he leads his Roman audience, and implicitly hopes to lead his presently unbelieving Jewish compatriots, to the worship of the God, who, in his sovereignty over all things and in his plan for the salvation of all, brought forth the Messiah from the Jewish people.[15]

---

13. Barr, "'*Abba* Isn't Daddy," 28–47. "Apart from leaving *abba* untranslated (which may be the best solution), perhaps 'dearest father' is nearer the meaning, because it emphasizes the respect and intimacy while also avoiding the overly sentimental connotations" (Burke, *Adopted into God's Family*, 95). "'Abba' was the regular Aramaic word for a male parent used both by adults and children. . . . At the very least, a liturgical context is implied by this Aramaic term that 'we' cry out together" (Jewett, *Romans*, 499).

14. "The Spirit appeals 'on behalf of the saints,' to be sure; but he does so always as one who, as very God, makes the appeal in keeping with God's will and his ways. Hence the one who leads us in the ways of God, demonstrating that we are indeed children of God (v. 14), is pictured as appealing in our behalf with the language of and in conformity to heaven. Rather than seeing praying in the Spirit as some sort of mindless activity, Paul sees it as a highly significant expression of prayer. In it the believer can take special encouragement even in the midst of present exigencies, for the Spirit is praying in keeping with God's will and with 'inarticulate groanings' that God himself well understands, since he knows the mind of the Spirit" (Fee, *God's Empowering Presence*, 586).

15. Regarding the particulars in the complex grammatical issue of whether the doxology in 9:5 is directed to Christ or to God, see Fee, *Pauline Christology*, 272–77. He concludes, "Pauline emphases both in Romans as a whole and in the present passage in particular (chs. 9–11) are so thoroughly theocentric that one would seem to need more than simply a single grammatical option to overturn that emphasis in this

Indeed, Paul indicates that any presently unbelieving Jew has everything necessary and readily available in the gospel (10:8) about this Jewish Christ to become a believer. Although the power of sin prevents proper worship with the "mouth" (3:14, 19), Paul invites every unbelieving Jew to become a worshiping believer and gain the hope for eternal salvation, as he declares, "If you confess with your *mouth* that Jesus is Lord and believe in your heart that God raised him from the dead, you will be saved. For with the heart a person believes for righteousness, and with the *mouth* a person confesses for salvation" (10:9–10). Such an individual confession preeminently takes place publicly within the liturgical assembly of the community of fellow believers.[16]

Paul is convinced and wants to convince his Roman audience that eventually, in accord with the mysterious plan of God, "all Israel will be saved!" (11:26).[17] He explains that, with regard to the gospel, presently unbelieving Jews are enemies of God for the sake of bringing Gentiles to faith; but with regard to their election they are beloved by God because of the patriarchs. For, as Paul insists, the gifts and the call of God are irrevocable. Just as presently believing Gentiles were once disobedient to God, but now have received mercy because of the disobedience of the Jews, so also presently unbelieving Jews have now been disobedient for the benefit of the mercy shown to Gentiles, in order that the Jews may now receive mercy. For God has imprisoned all in disobedience, in order that he may have mercy on all! (11:28–32).

Having disclosed this profound mystery whereby God, in and through his marvelous mercy, will bring all, Gentiles as well as Jews, to final salvation, Paul leads his Roman audience in an impressive act of worship that concludes the first eleven chapters of the letter with a magnificently inspiring liturgical climax. First, with the aid of pertinent

---

letter. . . . It would seem strikingly strange for Paul, as a climax to this list of Jewish privileges in a very Jewish context, to bless the *Messiah* as God when a doxology to God for all these privileges seems to be much more fitting" (275). "The 'Amen' at the end of this provocative but hopeful blessing invites the congregation to make it 'operative' by its assent" (Jewett, *Romans*, 569).

16. "But the emphasis is on 'heart' and 'mouth,' both of which stand in the emphatic position at the beginning of their clauses. Righteousness by Faith works its miracle first within the heart, convincing it of the love of God (5:5, 8) conveyed to the undeserving in the Christ event, and thereafter evokes the oral confession, "Lord Jesus!'" (Jewett, *Romans*, 569).

17. Zoccali, "'And So All Israel Will Be Saved,'" 289–318.

rhetorical questions taken from scripture, this act of worship praises God for the wisdom, knowledge, and intelligence of his ways. Then, following the example of Abraham, who gave glory to God (4:20), as the father of all who believe, both Jews and Gentiles (4:11–12), Paul brings this exhilarating act of worship to its climax with a rousing ritualistic doxology. Listen now to its resounding hymnic power: "O the depth of the riches and wisdom and knowledge of God! How unsearchable his decisions and inscrutable his ways! For, who has known the mind of the Lord, or who has been his adviser [Isa 40:13]? Or, who has given to him beforehand, so that he might be repaid [Job 35:7; 41:11]? For from him and through him and to him are all things! To him the glory forever! Amen!" (11:33–36).[18]

Ethical Worship in the Letter

Having led his Roman audience in this electrifying act of liturgical worship, Paul now leads them to a consideration of a corresponding ethical worship, as he immediately declares, "I exhort you then, brothers, by the mercies of God to present your bodies as a living sacrifice, holy and pleasing to God, your enlightened worship! Do not conform yourselves to this present age, but be continually transformed in the renewal of your mind, so that you may determine what is the will of God, what is good and pleasing and perfect!" (12:1–2).[19] As a consequence of all the

18. "The only thing that human beings may appropriately 'give' God is 'glory' (cf. 4:20c). The entire kerygmatic portion of the letter (1:16–11:36) thus ends with an invitation to give to God the recognition ('glory') which it is the essence of sin to refuse (1:21–23). God's dramatic intervention in Christ (3:21–26) has overcome the blockage thrown up by human sin, creating out of all nations—Jews and Gentiles—a people united in the common glorification of God, the supreme goal of human existence (15:8–12)" (Byrne, *Romans*, 360). "As in the two earlier occurrences of 'Amen' in Rom 1:25 and 9:5, Paul expects the congregation to confirm the specific theological point of his argument; there is explicit confirmation of such a liturgical expectation in 1 Cor 14:16 where Paul asks, 'how can anyone in the position of an outsider say the "Amen" to your thanksgiving when he does not know what you are saying?' So, in Rom 11:36, the congregation is invited to assent to the entire argument . . . including the controversial 'mystery' of Gentile and Jewish conversion" (Jewett, *Romans*, 723).

19. "The first two verses of Romans 12 place the concluding chapters of the letter under the umbrella of worship" (Peterson, *Engaging with God*, 178). For a reading of Romans 12 within a sociocultural context of a contemporary model house church, see Oakes, *Reading Romans in Pompeii*, 98–126.

many compassionate "mercies of God" that he has previously illustrated throughout the first eleven chapters of the letter, Paul exhorts his fellow believers to respond to this merciful grace of God with an ethical worship. That God has now graciously justified sinners through the "mercy" of his forgiveness (1:16–17; 3:21–4:25), has displayed the "mercy" of his love for us as sinners (5:1–11; 8:31–39), and that God "will have mercy" on all (11:32), including all Israel (11:26), as he has already bestowed his "mercy" on believers (9:15, 23–25; 11:30–32), exemplify the many "mercies of God" by which Paul stimulates his audience to gratefully offer their entire lives in an ethical worship of this God of mercy.

With a surprising twist on his figurative application of technical cultic terms to the new Christian way of life, Paul indicates the totally self-giving response to God's mercies—God's grace—that is now possible and appropriate from his Roman audience. They are to present not the bodies of dead animals but their own living bodies, their entire selves, their very own persons, as a "living sacrifice." Whereas sacrifices normally involved the destruction or death of something that is to be set apart and consecrated to God, Christians are to dedicate themselves, while still alive and in their everyday living, as an ethical "sacrifice" set apart to be "holy" and "pleasing" to God, as all cultic sacrifices were meant to be.[20]

In contrast to the external, physical rites normally involved in the cultic service of sacrificing, this "pleasing" or "acceptable" sacrificial worship that Christians are to offer is to be an "enlightened" or "intelligent" worship. The phrase here translated as "enlightened worship" is often translated as "spiritual worship." But the Greek adjective is *logikos*, which has to do with the process of mental reasoning. Christians presenting themselves as living sacrifices can be called "enlightened worship," because such worship has been "enlightened" or made intelligent by the mercies of God, which disclose the mysterious wisdom,

20. "Paul describes the offering of believers' bodies as a 'living sacrifice' presumably in contrast to the animals and inanimate produce offered in sacrifice in the Jerusalem Temple or in the pagan shrines which Gentile Christians may have frequented before their conversion. The great prophets of Israel, especially Hosea, Isaiah and Jeremiah, frequently pointed out the meaninglessness of sacrifices unaccompanied by true inner conversion and commitment to social justice. They laid down criteria for what is and what is not sacrifice 'pleasing to God.' Paul stands within the broad flow of this tradition when he extends to life in the body the notion of a 'sacrifice' which God is truly pleased to receive from creatures" (Byrne, *Romans*, 363).

knowledge, and mind of God (11:33–34). That this is an "enlightened" or "intelligent" worship governed by the thinking that takes place in one's mind seems to be confirmed in the elaboration on it in the next verse, which speaks of being "transformed" by God (divine passive) "in the renewal of your mind" (12:2).

Paul previously exhorted his Roman audience to think of themselves as already "dead" to the destructive power of sin, but "living" to God (6:11). Christians can and must present themselves to God as those who have been brought from the hopelessness of being "dead" to the hope of "living" (6:13). They must now present the members of their bodies as slaves to God's righteousness which leads to their "holiness" by being sanctified by God (6:19). Similarly, Paul now urges his Roman audience to present themselves as a "living sacrifice," an ethical worship that is "holy" and pleasing to God (12:1).

Through this "enlightened" or "intelligent" worship of offering themselves to God, Christians are to be transformed by God in the renewal of their minds, so that they may determine what is the will of God for them in their everyday lives. This implies that petitionary prayer is key to this ethical worship, since, as already indicated by Paul (1:10), such prayers involve conforming one's own will to the will of God. Through this renewal of their minds Christians may also determine what is "good" and "pleasing" and "perfect" (12:2)—terms with cultic associations, which are now used to describe the acceptable ethical worship to be performed by Christians.[21]

Having exhorted his audience to an "enlightened" ethical worship, Paul then gives a number of examples of the sort of behavior this entails. Each member of the Roman audience is to be allowed to perform his or her particular charism or spiritual gift in order to thereby contribute to the entire community as the one body of Christ (12:3–8). There should be a warm, affectionate, and genuine love operative within this Christian community; Christians should love one another in, through, and for hope, which includes remaining constant in prayer (12:12); Christians should be caring, hospitable, compassionate, and friendly

---

21. Vahrenhorst, *Kultische Sprache*, 305; "Believers . . . have no need to go to a temple to offer sacrifice to God. Their 'renewed mind' creates in them the capacity to discern what is required to live according to God's will. The bodily obedience flowing from that discernment makes their lives a continual 'sacrifice' pleasing to God" (Byrne, *Romans*, 364–65). See also Matera, *Romans*, 287–88.

toward all; Christians should foster peace and never take revenge on others (12:9–20); Christians should be good citizens (13:1–7), should love rather than harm their neighbors (13:8–10), and conduct themselves uprightly in accord with their hope for salvation (13:11–14).

Paul then addresses a specific problem within the Roman Christian community that has ramifications for both their ethical and liturgical worship. The problem involves those whom Paul designates the "strong" as opposed to the "weak" in faith. The so-called "weak" in faith had scruples or weak consciences about eating certain foods, which they deemed to be unclean. These Christians may have been primarily but not exclusively those with a Jewish heritage. The so-called "strong" in faith were those Christians who had no scruples about eating such food. These "strong" in faith were not exclusively Gentile Christians; Paul included himself among them.

In this matter involving certain foods both the "strong" and the "weak" are able to properly worship God. As Paul points out, "whoever eats something, eats it in honor of the Lord, for he gives thanks to God. Likewise, whoever refuses to eat something, refuses to eat it in honor of the Lord and gives thanks to God" (14:6).[22]

But the "strong" should not judge or condemn the "weak." It will be good for the well-being of the Christian community for the "strong" to give up their right to eat the food in question, and not to do anything that will cause a fellow Christian to stumble in his faith (14:21). Paul insists that "we who are strong ought to bear the weaknesses of the weak and not please ourselves" (15:1), by following the example of Christ who did not please himself in the sufferings he endured (15:3). Paul then offers a prayer of petition for the community's renewed experience of God's grace in this matter, with a further indication of the way of thinking that is to be part of their "enlightened" or "intelligent" worship: "May the God of steadfastness and encouragement grant you to think among yourselves in the same way, according to Christ Jesus, so that together with one voice you may glorify the God and Father

---

22. "The context of 'eating/not eating' suggests that *eucharistein* here has specific reference to the grace accompanying meals, though a more general and fundamental sense of 'giving thanks to God' can hardly be excluded" (Byrne, *Romans*, 413). "If each group can acknowledge the devotion of the other, directed to the same Lord Jesus Christ, and giving thanks to the same God, they will be able to share their meals with each other without insisting on uniformity" (Jewett, *Romans*, 847).

of our Lord Jesus Christ!" (15:5–6). This prayer thus illustrates how a harmoniously unified Christian community is paramount for both the ethical and liturgical glorification of God.[23]

Paul's exhortation moves beyond the specific rift between the "strong" and the "weak" to the more general situation of the Christian community as composed of Jews and Gentiles. By skillfully demonstrating how Christ has already "welcomed" both the Jews and Gentiles among his audience (15:8–9), Paul persuasively prods them to continue to play their respective and essential roles in "glorifying God," both ethically and liturgically, by warmly "welcoming" one another in Christian love for the sake of God's glory (15:7).

That there can and must be a mutual respect and concern between Jews and Gentiles for the ethical and liturgical glory of God, Paul dazzlingly illustrates with a striking and dramatically constructed series of hymnic scriptural citations (15:9–12) meticulously woven together by a repeated occurrence of the word "Gentiles" and by various depictions of "glorifying" God. Whereas the first quotation (Ps 18:49) vibrantly portrays the praise of God by an individual Jew among Gentiles as a group, the second quotation (Deut 32:43) directly addresses these Gentiles and excitedly invites them to rejoice along with the group of God's people, Israel. The third quote (Ps 117:1) universalizes the invitation to "*all* the Gentiles" and to "*all* the peoples" to praise the Lord, the God of Israel. These stunning scriptural hymns prompt the Roman audience to a full participation in this global praising and glorifying of God that takes place in and through both their ethical and liturgical worship.[24]

Reaching the pinnacle of his encouraging exhortations regarding the ethical as well as liturgical worship of his Roman audience, Paul

23. "If all are bent upon 'pleasing' not themselves but the neighbor, then differences of view on matters such as food will not injure the fundamental unity. The community will be able to fulfill its ultimate goal, expressed in what would appear to be a liturgical formula. . . . the double insistence upon unity may imply a sense that differences over food can spill over into worship and prevent the community from truly worshiping God as one body" (Byrne, *Romans*, 426–27). "[I]t seems quite likely that liturgical formulas derived from the Jewish liturgy such as the threefold 'Holy, Holy, Holy' of Isa 6:3 sung by the angelic choir are in view here. As humans participate in this chorus of praise, sharing the pleasing euphony of the benediction itself, God's glory is extended and increased" (Jewett, *Romans*, 885).

24. Malan, "Church Singing," 509–24; Heil, "Romans 15:7–13," 187–211.

climactically reinforces and sums them up with a zestful and zealous prayer for its accomplishment. Releasing a closing burst of burning enthusiasm, he ardently prays, "May the God of hope fill you with complete joy and peace in believing, so that you may abound in hope by the power of the Holy Spirit!" (15:13). He thus prays that the God who grants and sustains hope may fill his Roman audience with a complete joy and peace in their life of faith, which they, as a united Christian community of the "strong" and the "weak," of Gentiles and Jews, may actualize and experience in and through their liturgical as well as ethical worship.[25]

Paul's Apostolic Worship in the Letter

In concluding the letter, Paul explains the important role the Christians at Rome are yet to play in his apostolic hope for the future of his missionary activity (15:22–33), which he describes as a kind of "apostolic worship." He tells his Roman audience that he has written the letter to them because of the grace given to him by God "to be a minister (*leitourgon*) of Christ Jesus to the nations, serving the gospel of God like a priest (*heirourgounta*), so that the offering (*prosphora*) of the nations might be acceptable, consecrated in the Holy Spirit" (15:16).[26] With cultic imagery Paul thus describes his dedication to his task and privilege of preaching the gospel to all: He is a devoted "minister" of worship, who serves the gospel of God like a "priest" assigned to perform worship in the temple, so that the "offering" or "sacrifice," which consists in the various nations coming to faith in the gospel, might be "acceptable"

25. "The missional goal remains in sharp focus right to the end of this eloquent benediction, while the concluding phrase makes it a performative blessing, conveyed and empowered by the spirit as the letter is being read aloud in the worship services of the Roman congregations. With this magnificent ending of the formal argumentation in the letter, Paul can now move into his peroration, taking up the practical steps that are required to bring this world-transforming mission to fulfillment" (Jewett, *Romans*, 899).

26. "God sends Paul as a minister of Christ Jesus to the Gentiles (Rom 15:16). His job is to be a *leitourgos*, which in itself implies no cultic functions; but he goes on to say 'for the *heirourgia* of the gospel,' so his is in fact a sacred ministry and, more than that, a priestly function. Paul's whole apostolate is conceived as a *leitourgia*" (Spicq, "*leitourgeō*," 382–83). See also Matera, *Romans*, 332–33.

to God and "consecrated" by the Holy Spirit, like a cultic sacrifice that was to be consecrated and acceptable to God.[27]

As the Christians at Rome play a pivotal role in Paul's apostolic hope for extending the gospel as far as Spain (15:24), so they must also assist him in his apostolic hope for successfully delivering the collection to the mother church in Jerusalem. Paul urgently exhorts his Roman audience to share in his hope for the success of the Jerusalem ministry by praying before God on his behalf. They are to join in his hope by striving together with him as they actualize their hope in their prayers (15:30). Their own prayers of petition for Paul that his sacrificial service for the Christians in Jerusalem may be "acceptable" (15:31) will thus reciprocally complement Paul's making mention of them always in his prayers of petition, "begging that somehow, sometime, at last I may succeed by God's will to come to you" (1:10). Paul then punctuates his request for their prayers with his own prayerful greeting for them without an explicit verb, so that it can be heard comprehensively in a past, present and future way, namely, "The God of peace has been, is now, and always will be with you all! Amen!" (15:33).[28]

---

27. "The cultic language is, of course, metaphorical and reflects the tendency of the early Christian community to apply to itself as eschatological people of God terminology and imagery taken from Israel's worship. Paul is not portraying himself as 'priest' in the sense of the distinction between ordained clergy and laity that arose much later in Christian usage. In terms of the original image taken from the ritual of sacrifice, the presence and operation of the priest as God's minister ensures that what is offered is acceptable to the deity" (Byrne, *Romans*, 435–36). "Paul's evangelistic proclamation results in a transformation of the Gentiles into 'an acceptable offering' in the fulfillment of an end-time scheme announced in 11:11, 25 and derived from Isa 66:20. Paul uses a term for a sacrificial or votive offering, *prosphora*, a word with a technical liturgical meaning in the LXX" (Jewett, *Romans*, 907).

28. "The 'amen' in Rom 15:33 has a function similar to the use earlier in the letter (1:25), inviting the Roman audience to add its concurrence by a liturgical response to what Paul has just said. They are expected to reply to Paul's 'amen' with an 'amen' of their own. The 'so be it' function of this liturgical formula confirms God's peace as uniting both the Roman believers and their fellow members from various ethnic traditions throughout the world. The benediction followed by 'amen' thus provides an appropriate transition to the introduction of Phoebe and the requests for mutual greetings in the rest of chapter 16, affirming the need of God's peace within the church so that the gospel may be able to extend the realm of divine concord to the end of the known world" (Jewett, *Romans*, 940).

Worship in the Letter's Closing

Even within the list of personal greetings that closes the letter Paul acts as a leader of worship. He especially commends to his audience in Rome a certain Phoebe, designated as "our sister," a "deaconess" or "helper" of the Christian community in Cenchreae, an eastern seaport for Corinth. Since Paul is probably composing the letter from Corinth, it may well be that Phoebe has been entrusted to deliver the letter and arrange for its public performance within a gathering for worship. They are to provide her whatever she needs from them for her work at hand, possibly that involved in delivering the letter (16:1–2).[29] He also bids the Christians at Rome to extend greetings to Prisca and Aquila, his fellow workers in spreading the gospel of Christ Jesus.[30] They have previously gone so far as to risk their lives to assist Paul in his apostolate. For this reason not only Paul himself but all the Gentile churches he founded in the Mediterranean area are engaged in the worship of thanking God (16:3–4; cf. 1:8, 21; 14:6).

Before closing the letter, Paul directs the Romans, whom he has been leading in worship throughout the letter, to greet one another with a "holy kiss" as a gesture of fraternal esteem and affection appropriate for their communal worship (16:16).[31] He then adds his own brief

29. Arichea, "Who Was Phoebe?," 401–9; Jewett, "Paul, Phoebe, and the Spanish Mission," 144–64; Romaniuk, "Was Phoebe in Romans 16,1 a Deaconess?"132–34; Schulz, "A Case for 'President' Phoebe in Romans 16:2," 124–27; Whelan, "Role of Phoebe," 67–85. "Ancient epistolary practice would therefore assume that the recommendation of Phoebe was related to her task of conveying and interpreting the letter in Rome as well as in carrying out the business entailed in the letter" (Jewett, *Romans*, 943).

30. Lampe, *Die städtrömischen Christen*, 156–64. "The first persons to be greeted are Prisca and Aquila, who had worked with Paul in his earlier missions in Corinth and Ephesus. It is clear from Acts 18:2 that both of them were banned from Rome at the time of the Edict of Claudius in 49 C.E., which means that they were not Pauline converts in Corinth but had been leaders in the Roman church prior to meeting Paul for the first time. At the time of writing 1 Cor 16:19, Paul sent greetings to the Corinthians from Prisca and Aquila's church in Ephesus. The greeting in Romans makes it clear that they have now returned to Rome, probably after the lapse of the Edict of Claudius in 54" (Jewett, *Romans*, 954–55).

31. "Since the holy kiss was associated with the celebration of the love feast, which probably occurred each time congregations met, the admonition entails the obligation to welcome one another into full fellowship and worship" (Jewett, *Romans*, 974). See also Klassen, "Sacred Kiss in the New Testament," 122–35.

prayerful greeting that recalls the one that initiated the ritualistic worship of the letter (1:7), thus placing the entire letter within a context of prayerful worship, as he exclaims that the grace of our Lord Jesus has been, is now, and always will be with you! (16:20).

The dramatic doxology that now closes the letter as a ritual of worship skillfully sums up its key points in a splendid act of inspiring worship. Paul's purpose for the letter was to spiritually "strengthen" and encourage the Roman Christians (1:11–12), who already possess the "obedience of faith," which is the goal of Paul's apostolate to the nations (1:5). This spiritual strength has its firm foundation in Paul's "gospel," as the definitive and decisive unfolding of the "mystery" now disclosed and made evident through the prophetic writings (1:1–2; 3:21). This "mystery" (11:25) includes how God in the depth of his "wisdom" (11:33) will bring all, Gentiles as well as Jews, to final salvation by means of his marvelous mercy (11:26, 32).

In conclusion, listen to how appropriately Paul, through this final doxology, leads his audience to respond to the entire letter with a climactic act of glorious worship: "To him who has the power to strengthen you according to my gospel and the preaching of Jesus Christ, according to the revelation of the mystery kept secret for long ages, but now manifested and made known through the prophetic writings in accord with the command of the eternal God for the obedience of faith among all the nations—to the only wise God, through Jesus Christ, glory forever! Amen!" (16:25–27).[32]

---

32. For a defense of the authenticity of Rom 16:25–27, which most interpreters consider to be a later interpolation, see Hurtado, "Doxology at the End of Romans," 185–99. The doxology in 16:25–27 is taken as part of the letter's closing by Weima: "The doxology is, in fact, especially striking for the way in which it recapitulates the concern of Paul evident in the epistolary framework of the letter" (*Neglected Endings*, 219). "Perhaps alluding to Paul's own sustained exclamation of praise in 11:33–36, the doxology then resumes the summons to praise God as 'only wise.' As set forth in Paul's letter to Rome, God has worked out in Christ a plan of salvation for humankind that no merely human mind or imagination could have anticipated or framed. The God who acted inclusively to bring formerly excluded Gentiles within the salvation promised to the human race through Israel will likewise act inclusively to bring that bulk of Israel presently excluded from salvation within the same inclusive scope of salvation. Gentile hearers, knowing themselves to be caught up irrevocably within the grasp of this unfolding plan, can only respond, 'Amen!'" (Byrne, *Romans*, 463).

Conclusion: Worship in Romans

To sum up, at this point we have explored Paul's letter to the Romans by examining it as an epistolary ritual of worship. It was publicly presented and delivered orally within the context of a liturgical assembly to the ecclesial community of Christians at Rome, probably as they gathered in various house churches. In it Paul not only performed his own acts of worship, which included thanksgiving, prayerful petition, and praise, but exhorted, invited, and led his audience to do the same. Listening to the letter inspired and motivated the worship of these Roman believers, not only their liturgical but also their ethical worship.

Paul addresses the letter to all those in Rome, beloved of God and called as "holy ones" (1:7a), that is, as those who have been set apart by God and consecrated for the worship of God. Paul's opening greeting to them (1:7b) initiates the ritualistic worship of the letter and establishes a liturgical tone for it. Paul then performs an epistolary act of worship, a thanksgiving in response to divine grace (1:8), modelling for his Roman audience how the grace and peace available to them is to spark their worship of God through Jesus Christ as a response of respectful, reverent, and joyous gratitude.

Paul leads the audience into a true and proper worship of God as the Creator by extolling God as the one "who is blessed forever! Amen!" (1:25). Paul thus draws his audience into this poignant act of ritualistic worship, as his reverent benediction, exuberantly reinforced by a liturgically resounding "Amen!," is intended to generate his fellow Roman believers' own reverberating benediction and reaffirming "Amen!" In contrast to the false worship of the ungodly, who exchanged the "glory" of the immortal God for an image of mortal man (1:23), and to all who are unable to worship because the power of sin has deprived them of the "glory" of God (3:23), Abraham "gave glory" to the God who gives life to the dead. He thus stands as a stellar model of worship for all who believe and have hope in the God who raised Jesus our Lord from the dead (4:24).

A ritualistic act of worship, the sacrament of baptism, makes possible the ethical or moral worship of Christians. Paul pointedly informs his audience that when we were ritually baptized as Christians, we all sacramentally participated and shared in the actual death of Jesus

Christ. We were "buried," that is, totally and definitively immersed, with him by our baptism into his death. Since we were sacramentally joined with him in his death, we may also now live a new life, a life that includes ethical worship.

Although, according to Paul, those who live in the flesh cannot please God (8:8), we believers, as those who have received the Spirit of sonship, are able to cry out in the liturgical assembly with an exclamation of an intimately filial worship, "Abba! Father!" (8:15). We are able to relate to, please, and worship God as God's very own children, who have the hope of being glorified with Christ (8:16). Paul assures us that as we pray for it, the Spirit of God intercedes for us with wordless groanings to ensure that we pray in accord with the will of God (8:26–27).

Paul is convinced and wants to convince his Roman audience that eventually, in accord with the mysterious plan of God, "all Israel will be saved!" (11:26). Having disclosed this profound mystery whereby God, in and through his marvelous mercy, will bring all, Gentiles as well as Jews, to final salvation, Paul leads his Roman audience in an impressive act of worship that concludes the first eleven chapters of the letter with a magnificently inspiring liturgical climax (11:33–36).

Through an "enlightened" or "intelligent" worship of offering themselves to God, Christians are to be transformed by God in the renewal of their minds, so that they may determine what is the will of God for them in their everyday lives. This implies that petitionary prayer is key to this ethical worship, since, as already indicated by Paul (1:10), such prayers involve conforming one's own will to the will of God. Through this renewal of their minds Christians may also determine what is "good" and "pleasing" and "perfect" (12:2)—terms with cultic associations, which are now used to describe the acceptable ethical worship to be performed by Christians.

Paul offers a prayer of petition for the community's renewed experience of God's grace regarding a division between the "strong" and "weak" among them, with a further indication of the way of thinking that is to be part of their "enlightened" or "intelligent" worship (15:5–6). This prayer thus illustrates how a harmoniously unified Christian community is paramount for both the ethical and liturgical glorification of God. Paul prays that the God who grants and sustains hope may fill his Roman audience with a complete joy and peace in their life of faith

(15:7–13), which they, as a united Christian community of the "strong" and the "weak," of Gentiles and Jews, may actualize and experience in and through their liturgical as well as ethical worship.

With cultic imagery Paul describes his dedication to his task and privilege of preaching the gospel to all: He is a devoted "minister" of worship, who serves the gospel of God like a "priest" assigned to perform worship in the temple, so that the "offering" or "sacrifice" that consists in the various nations coming to faith in the gospel might be "acceptable" to God and "consecrated" by the Holy Spirit, like a cultic sacrifice that was to be consecrated and acceptable to God. Paul urgently exhorts his Roman audience to share in his hope for the success of the Jerusalem ministry by praying before God on his behalf (15:30). Their own prayers of petition for Paul that his sacrificial service for the Christians in Jerusalem may be "acceptable" (15:31) will thus reciprocally complement Paul's making mention of them always in his prayers of petition, "begging that somehow, sometime, at last I may succeed by God's will to come to you" (1:10). Paul then punctuates his request for their prayers with his own prayerful greeting for them (15:33).

Before closing the letter, Paul directs the Romans, whom he has been leading in worship throughout the letter, to greet one another with a "holy kiss" as a gesture of fraternal esteem and affection appropriate for their communal worship (16:16). He then adds his own brief prayerful greeting, which recalls the one that initiated the ritualistic worship of the letter (1:7), thus placing the entire letter within a context of prayerful worship, as he exclaims that the grace of our Lord Jesus has been, is now, and always will be with you! (16:20). The dramatic doxology that climactically closes the letter as a ritual of worship skillfully sums up its key points in a magnificent act of inspiring worship (16:25–27).

Philemon

Paul's letter to Philemon was sent to the church that gathered at the house of Philemon, probably located in the city of Colossae, since the Onesimus mentioned in the letter as the slave of Philemon (Phlm 1:10) is most likely the same Onesimus described in the letter to the Colossians as "one of you" (Col 4:9). In addition there are several other names of individuals mentioned in both of these letters (cf. Phlm 1:2, 23–24; Col 4:10–17). Paul is in prison (Phlm 1:1, 10, 13, 23) when he and Timothy send the letter to Philemon, so that it is numbered among the Pauline "captivity" letters, in addition to Colossians, Ephesians, Philippians, and 2 Timothy. Since there is no mention in Philemon of the possibility of Paul's imminent execution, as there is in both Philippians and 2 Timothy, and, indeed, since Paul hopes to be released and to visit Philemon (1:22), it seems likely that Paul is imprisoned in Caesarea, rather than Rome, when he sends the letter to Philemon. Paul may well have sent Tychicus not only with the letters to the Colossians (Col 4:7) and to the Ephesians (Eph 6:21) from his Caesarean imprisonment but also with the letter to Philemon.[1]

---

1. According to the Acts of the Apostles, Paul's mission in Jerusalem did not go as well as he had hoped in his letter to the Romans (Rom 15:22–33). Indeed, Jews in Jerusalem tried to seize and kill him. Eventually he was arrested by the Roman military and imprisoned in Caesarea, where he was held in custody for some time (Acts 20:22—26:32). After his adventurous sea journey from Caesarea to Rome he remained imprisoned there as he awaited his trial before Caesar (Acts 27–28). These circumstances may well have resulted in the cancellation of Paul's plans for apostolic ministry in Spain after visiting the Christian community in Rome (Rom 15:24, 28). At any rate, it appears that Paul was imprisoned long enough in Caesarea, at least two years (Acts 24:27), to compose and send the letters to Philemon, to the Colossians, and to the Ephesians.

The letter to Philemon centers around the change in relationship that has occurred between Philemon and his slave Onesimus, whom the imprisoned Paul converted to the Christian faith. Although Philemon is the primary recipient, the letter is a communal one, addressed to and heard by the entire church assembled at his house. Since the letter is very brief, it can be presented in its entirety, as exhibiting the following chiastic structure:

A ¹ Paul a prisoner of *Christ Jesus* and Timothy the brother to Philemon *our* beloved and *fellow worker* ² and Apphia the sister and Archippus our fellow soldier and the assembly at your house. ³ *Grace* to *you* and peace from God our Father and the *Lord Jesus Christ.*

> B ⁴ I *thank* my God every time I make mention of you in my *prayers,* ⁵ hearing of your love and faith, which you have toward the *Lord* Jesus and for all the holy ones, ⁶ that the partnership of your faith might become effective in the recognition of all the good that is among us for *Christ.* ⁷ *For* I have had much joy and encouragement in *your love,* because *the hearts* of the holy ones have been *refreshed through* you, *brother.*

> > C ⁸ Therefore, though having much boldness in Christ to command to *you* what is proper, ⁹ on account of love I would rather appeal, being as I am, *Paul,* an old man and now also a prisoner of Christ Jesus. ¹⁰ I appeal to *you* for *my* child, whom I have begotten in prison, Onesimus,

> > > D ¹¹ who was once *to you* "useless" but now is indeed both *to you* and *to me* "useful," ¹² whom I am sending back *to you, him,* that is *my* heart, ¹³ whom *I* wanted to *keep* for myself, so that he might serve on *your* behalf *me* in the imprisonment of the gospel,

> > > > E ¹⁴ but without your consent I resolved to do nothing, so that your good might not be as under compulsion but rather under benevolence.

> > > D′ ¹⁵ For perhaps it was for this reason he was separated for awhile, so that you might have *him back* forever, ¹⁶ no longer as a slave but more than a slave, a beloved brother, especially *to me,* but how much more *to you* both in the flesh and in the Lord. ¹⁷ If then you have *me* as a partner, welcome *him* as *me.*

C′ ¹⁸ And if he has wronged *you* in anyway or owes you anything, charge it *to me*. ¹⁹ I, *Paul*, am writing in my own hand, I will repay; but may I not say to *you* that you more than owe me your very self!

B′ ²⁰ Yes, *brother*, may I "benefit" from you in the *Lord; refresh* my *heart* in *Christ*. ²¹ Confident of *your obedience* I am writing to you, knowing that you will do even more than I say. ²² And at the same time also prepare for me a guest room; *for* I am hoping that *through* your *prayers I will be granted* to you.

A′ ²³ Epaphras, my fellow captive in *Christ Jesus*, greets you, ²⁴ as well as Mark, Aristarchus, Demas, and Luke, my *fellow workers*. ²⁵ The *grace* of the *Lord Jesus Christ* be with *your* spirit.

It is sometimes maintained that precisely what Paul wants of Philemon is unclear. The chiastic structure of the letter, however, indicates not only what Paul wants from Philemon, namely, Onesimus (not necessarily as freed from slavery) to serve on his behalf in the work of the gospel (v. 13), but also why he wants it, namely, as a further "good" that Philemon can do under benevolence (v. 14) for Paul and the holy ones based on love and in response to divine grace.

In the A unit (vv. 1–3) of the chiasm Paul's greeting as a prisoner of Christ Jesus places the audience of the letter, as they listen to it within a liturgical assembly, within a framework of God's grace. In response to this grace Paul in the B unit (vv. 4–7) thanks God in his prayers for Philemon's faithful love toward the holy ones, suggesting that as partners they can do a further "good" for Christ. On the basis of love Paul as an old man and prisoner of Christ Jesus appeals for his "child" Onesimus in the C unit (vv. 8–10). In the D unit (vv. 11–13) Paul indicates that he would like Onesimus, his very heart, who as a Christian has become "useful" to both Philemon and Paul, to serve Paul on behalf of Philemon in the work of the gospel. The first half of the chiasm reaches its climax in the E unit (v. 14) with Paul's resolve that the "good" that Philemon can do in granting him Onesimus be under benevolence.

As the center and pivotal point of the chiasm, the E unit (v. 14) serves as the dominant motivation for the development of Paul's appeal in the second half. Through inverse parallelism with the D unit, in which Paul wants to keep Onesimus for himself, the D′ unit (vv. 15–17) suggests that Philemon can have Onesimus back forever by giving him back to Paul after welcoming him as a beloved brother and as a partner like Paul himself. In the C' unit (vv. 18–19) Paul himself offers to pay any debts of his "child" for whom he appealed in the C unit, Onesimus, but reminds Philemon that he more than owes Paul his very self, thus suggesting Onesimus as payment. Paul, in the B' unit (vv. 20–22), wants his "brother" Philemon to refresh his heart (Onesimus), as he refreshed the hearts of the holy ones in the B unit; in reciprocal and complementary correspondence to Paul's prayers of thanks for grace (B unit), Paul hopes through the prayers of the assembly to be granted to them from grace as further motivation and occasion for Philemon to graciously grant Onesimus to Paul (B' unit). The greetings of grace to the entire assembly that frame the letter in the A (vv. 1–3) and A' (vv. 23–25) units provide the ultimate motivation for Philemon to grant Onesimus to Paul for service to the gospel of Christ under the benevolence of grace.[2]

Philemon as a Ritual of Worship

In the letter to Philemon Paul draws the liturgical assembly, gathered together in the house of Philemon (v. 2), into his worship of "thanking" (*eucharistō*) God (v. 4) for the "grace" (*charis*) that comes from God the Father and the Lord Jesus Christ (v. 3), as he prays that Philemon recognize all the "good" that can be done for Christ as part of this grateful worship (v. 6). Based on a new manifestation of the grace of God evident in his slave, Onesimus, becoming a fellow believer (vv. 10–11) and thus "brother" (v. 16), Philemon, out of love, can do the "good" of allowing Onesimus to serve Paul in advancing the gospel of Christ (v. 14). By doing this "good" in obedience to God, Philemon can deepen the liturgical assembly's experience of the grace of God as the focus of their grateful worship. Indeed, that Paul has resolved to do nothing without the consent of Philemon, so that his "good" might not be as under compulsion but rather under "benevolence (*hekousion*)" (v. 14), that is, voluntarily or of his free will, underlines how the "good" that Philemon can do in allowing him to rejoin Paul amounts to a sacrificial "free will offering" to God.[3]

2. Heil, "Philemon," 178–206.

3. The phrase "under benevolence" (*kata hekousion*) or "according to free will"

And the church in the house of Philemon may gain a further experience of God's grace, as the imprisoned Paul hopes that "I will be granted" (literally, "graced," *charisthēsomai*), by God to them through their prayers as a worshiping community (v. 22). The closing prayer-greeting, "the grace of the Lord Jesus Christ be with your (plural) spirit" (v. 25) forms a literary inclusion with the opening prayer-greeting, "grace to you (plural) and peace from God the Father and the Lord Jesus Christ" (v. 3), to envelope the entire letter within a context of communal worship. Paul thus ends the letter to Philemon with a prayer that the church in his house may continue to experience the divine grace they have already experienced (v. 3), and Paul hopes that they will continue to experience the effects of this saving grace through the "good" that Philemon can do for Onesimus, Paul, and his house church.[4]

---

occurs in a context of sacrificial worship in Num 15:3 (LXX): "You will make whole burnt offerings to the Lord, a whole burnt offering or sacrifice to make great a vow, or a free will offering (*kath' hekousion*)." The noun *hekousios* is the usual rendering for "a voluntary or free-will offering," according to Wevers (*Numbers*, 237). "*Hekousios* occurs only here in the NT but is widely used in the LXX to refer to 'freewill offerings,'" according to Moo (*Philemon*, 416n77). See also Fitzmyer, *Philemon*, 112.

4. "Paul extends this grace to Philemon's whole house church: the 'your' in *your spirit* is plural. A few interpreters have taken *pneuma* as a reference to the Holy Spirit, perhaps as indwelling the community as a whole. . . . The singular 'your spirit' is then distributive: the spirit that each of you has" (Moo, *Philemon*, 442).

Colossians

Some have questioned and/or denied that the historical apostle Paul could have authored Colossians because in their estimation it differs too greatly from the so-called main or undisputed letters of Paul.[1] This study, however, follows those scholars who argue that the Paul who is the primary author of the undisputed Pauline letters is also the primary author of the letter to the Colossians, which exhibits several similarities indicating a close relationship to the historical situation of the letter to Philemon, whose Pauline authorship is generally accepted.[2] But even those who maintain that the historical Paul is not the author of Colossians must admit that the letter itself presents Paul as its primary textual or implied author.

Paul is in prison (Col 4:3, 10, 18; cf. 1:24) when he and Timothy send the letter, so that Colossians is one of the Pauline "captivity" letters, in addition to Philemon, Ephesians, Philippians, and 2 Timothy. Rome, Ephesus, or Caesarea have been suggested as possible locations for Paul's imprisonment while authorizing and directing the composition of Colossians. It seems plausible that Paul sent Tychicus with the letter to the Colossians from his Caesarean imprisonment with both the letter to Philemon and the letter to the Ephesians. All three of these

---

1. See, for example, Kiley, *Colossians as Pseudepigraphy*.

2. Thompson, *Colossians & Philemon*, 2–5. "I will refer to the author of the letter as Paul because I believe that, in spite of the difficulties, the letter can still best be explained as written or authorized by Paul during his own lifetime" (ibid., 4). Smith, *Heavenly Perspective*, 6–16. "It is concluded that there is insufficient evidence to deny Pauline authorship of Colossians" (ibid., 16). "It remains one of the singular mysteries in NT scholarship that so many scholars reject Pauline authorship of Colossians yet affirm the authenticity of Philemon" (Fee, *Pauline Christology*, 289n2)

letters appear to be very closely related.[3] At any rate, that the implied author "Paul" was in prison somewhere for its composition and sending plays a significant role in the interpretation of Colossians.[4]

Paul and Timothy address the recipients of the letter as fellow believers set apart from the world and consecrated to God: they are "the holy ones and faithful brothers in Christ in Colossae" (1:2).[5] They have faith in Christ Jesus as well as love for all of their fellow believers, their fellow "holy ones" (1:4; 2:5). They have already heard of the hope reserved for them in heaven through the gospel (1:5) they learned from Epaphras, an associate of Paul and Timothy, "our beloved fellow slave, who is a faithful minister of Christ on behalf of you" (1:7).

The Colossian audience were probably mainly believers of Gentile origin whom God has made "fit for the share of the inheritance of the holy ones in the light" (1:12). They were once alienated from God and hostile of mind in evil deeds (1:21), "dead" in transgressions and in the "uncircumcision" of their flesh (2:13). Indeed, they formerly lived (3:7) in immorality, impurity, passion, evil desire, the greed that is idolatry (3:5), anger, fury, malice, slander, obscene language, and lying (3:8–9),

---

3. "The remarkable correspondence in personal names between Philemon and Colossians supports the conclusion that Colossians was also written during Paul's two-year imprisonment (A.D. 59–60) in Caesarea (Acts 24:27). . . . Chronologically, Ephesians may have been written somewhat later than Philemon and Colossians since Timothy is not mentioned. But A. D. 59 must still be the year of composition, because Tychicus was expected to take all three letters with him, delivering the letters to Philemon and to the Colossians in Colossae, before continuing on with Ephesians (cf. Col. 4:7—Tychicus with Philemon's servant Onesimus in 4:9, who was returned to Colossae—and Eph. 6:21, where Tychicus is still mentioned but not Onesimus)" (Reicke, *Paul's Letters*, 75, 83). See also Reicke, "Historical Setting," 429–38. On Caesarea as the origin of Colossians, see also Robinson, *Redating*, 65–67. With regard to the possibility that Paul sent Colossians while imprisoned in Caesarea, Thompson (*Colossians*, 6) states, "One might note here the interesting, but not complete, overlap between the names of coworkers in Colossians and those who accompanied Paul, particularly as he journeyed towards Jerusalem and subsequent detention in Caesarea (Aristarchus, Acts 19:29; 20:4; 27:2; Timothy and Tychicus, 20:4; see also Acts 12:12, 25; 15:37, 39 for references to Mark; 4:36; 9:27–15:39 *passim* for Barnabas)." See also Ellis, *History and Interpretation*, 86; idem, *Making of the New Testament*, 266–75.

4. On the significance of Paul being in prison for the interpretation of Colossians, but arguing for an imprisonment in Rome, see Cassidy, *Paul in Chains*, 88–94.

5. Colossae, together with the nearby cities of Laodicea and Hierapolis (cf. 4:13), was located in the Lycus river valley in the region of Phrygia in Asia Minor. The archaeological site now located in modern Turkey remains unexcavated. For a recent discussion of Colossae, see Wilson, *Colossians*, 3–6.

but have now been reconciled through the death of Christ in the body of his flesh (1:22). Yet this audience of former Gentiles seems to be familiar with some of the practices of Jews and probably also included former Jews, as indicated by the references to circumcision (2:11) and sabbaths (2:16), as well as allusions to scripture.[6]

Included in the audience of the letter are husbands and their wives, parents and their children, masters and their slaves (3:18–4:1), a certain "Nympha and the church in her house" (4:15), as well as Archippus, who is to fulfill the ministry he received in the Lord (4:17; cf. Phlm 1:2). Although the primary audience of the letter are the Colossian believers, it is meant to be read also to the believers in Laodicea (4:16; cf. 2:1; 4:13), and possibly by those in nearby Hierapolis as well (4:13), so that it can be considered a kind of circular letter addressed primarily to the Colossians, but relevant also to those in Laodicea and Hierapolis.

These implied audiences of believers are apparently in danger of being captivated "through a philosophy that is of empty deceit" (2:8). There has been much discussion about the precise nature of this "philosophy," with a great divergence of resulting theories and opinions.[7] It has been persuasively argued that this "philosophy" is not really a "heresy."[8] This "philosophy," literally "love of wisdom," refers broadly to a world view that embraces a "wise" way of living. It likely refers to the erroneous viewpoints and practices of some Jews in the local synagogues in the areas around Colossae and/or of some Jewish Christians influenced by them.[9] It evidently advocated ascetical practices and religious observances oriented to a mystical, heavenly worship of or with angels (2:16–18). The letter refutes any suggestion that believers in Christ lacked an authentic and complete "wisdom." It encourages them

6. "It would appear that the Christian church in Colossae was made up of both Jews and Gentiles. The Jewish influence within the congregation can be seen by references to circumcision (2.11) and to Sabbath (2.16). There are also allusions to a Gentile background for other members of the congregation. In 1.12, 21; 2.13 there are indications of outsiders being brought into the company of the people of God" (Smith, *Heavenly Perspective*, 5). See also Beetham, *Echoes of Scripture*.

7. Wilson, *Colossians*, 35–58.

8. Hooker, "False Teachers in Colossae?" 315–31.

9. Sappington, *Revelation*, 17–22; Harrington, "Christians and Jews in Colossians," 153–61; Dunn, "Colossian Philosophy," 153–81; idem, *Colossians*, 29–35; Garland, *Colossians*, 23–32; Bevere, *Sharing*; Thompson, *Colossians*, 6–9; Stettler, "Opponents," 169–200; Smith, *Heavenly Perspective*; Sumney, *Colossians*, 10–12.

"to walk," that is, to live, "in all wisdom"—rather than in a "philosophy of empty deceit," as "holy ones," those specially consecrated by God for the service and worship of God, "who are in Christ."[10]

Colossians as a Ritual of Worship

Introductory Worship

By describing "those in Colossae" as "holy ones" (1:2), Paul is making his audience aware that God has set them, like his chosen people of Israel of old, apart from the rest of the world and consecrated them for special benefits from and service—including liturgical and ethical worship—to God.[11] The audience are to realize that whereas Paul has been set apart through the will of God to be an apostle of Christ Jesus (1:1), God has also set them apart to be "holy ones" consecrated for the worship of God.[12]

Paul's greeting of God's "grace" (*charis*) to "you," his Colossian audience, expresses his prayer that God, who has already graced the audience in making them holy ones and believers in Christ, will grant them yet further divine grace, during and as a result of their listening to the letter itself.[13] This concept of the "grace" or "favor" of God is thus not only a gift from God but carries with it a connotation of divine empowerment or enablement. God's grace has empowered the audi-

---

10. Heil, *Colossians*.

11. "The substantive ('the holy ones') derives from the cultic idea of holiness as a being 'set apart from everyday usage, dedicated to God.' That idea of holiness was familiar in Hellenistic cults, but otherwise it is a characteristic and overwhemingly Jewish category. . . . What is striking, therefore, is that Paul felt able to incorporate into this distinctively Jewish self-description small gatherings of predominantly Gentile believers in Christ Jesus. The important inference is that Paul understood these Gentiles to have been incorporated into Israel, the people of God, through faith in and baptism in the name of Messiah Jesus—that is, without becoming Jewish proselytes (by being circumcised)" (Dunn, *Colossians*, 48).

12. "As God has made Paul his own as Christ's apostle, so God has made the Colossians as his covenant people in Colossae" (Garland, *Colossians*, 41).

13. "Paul's use of *charis* in his greetings indicates a deep prayerful concern (the element of intercession is present in the greetings) for the readers. He desires that the Colossians may apprehend more fully the grace of God in which they already stand" (O'Brien, *Colossians*, 5). "The letter itself is intended to be a means of grace, and the word reappears in the concluding wish in Colossians 4:18" (Garland, *Colossians*, 43).

ence to become holy ones and will empower them to live and worship as holy ones who are in Colossae; it has empowered them to become believers and will empower them to live and worship as believers who are in Christ (1:2). Coupled with God's grace that Paul prays to be given to his audience is "peace"—a state of overall well-being or harmony. Paul prays that with the grace of God his audience may live in peace with God, with one another as believers who are in Christ (1:2b), and, as holy ones and faithful brothers who are in Christ and in Colossae, with non-believers who are not in Christ but in Colossae (1:2a).[14]

In response to the initial greeting and prayer (1:2), Paul along with Timothy perform a reciprocal epistolary act of worship by giving thanks—"we thank" (*eucharistoumen*)—to God (1:3a) for the "grace" (*charis*) and peace that come *from* God our Father. The additional prayer report that Paul and Timothy thank the God and Father of our Lord Jesus Christ "always when praying for *you*" (1:3b) reinforces the previous prayer that "grace and peace from God our Father be with *you*" (1:2).[15] It further strengthens the bond between the senders and audience of the letter, making the Colossians aware not only of Paul and Timothy's appreciative gratitude but their prayerful concern for them.[16]

From the very day the audience heard of the grace of God in truth—in the word of the truth of the gospel (1:5–6)—the gospel has been bearing fruit and growing among them (1:6b). Correspondingly, *from the very day* Paul and Timothy heard of the audience's faith and love motivated by hope (1:4–5, 8), they do not cease praying on behalf of the audience (1:9a). This develops their previous worship of thanking

14. "The richness of the Jewish greeting 'peace' should not be lost sight of since it denotes not simply cessation of war but all that makes for well-being and prosperity in the absence of war, and not simply individual or inner peace, but also the social wholeness of harmonious relationships" (Dunn, *Colossians*, 51).

15. With regard to the significance of the adverb "always" here O'Brien (*Colossians*, 10) points out that it does not refer "to unceasing thanksgiving. To speak of prayer by this and similar terms (e.g. 'continually', 'at all times', 'day and night') was part and parcel of the style of ancient letters, being a Jewish practice as well as a pagan one. A measure of hyberbole is also to be noted in these expressions."

16. "At the beginning of most of his letters, in the formal thanksgiving period, the apostle assures his readers not only of his continual thanksgivings for them, but also of his constant intercessions on their behalf, and he indicates briefly some of the contents of his prayers" (Wiles, *Paul's Intercessory Prayers*, 156). "Paul saw his prayers not as a substitute for their own prayers but as a natural expression of Christian love and concern" (Dunn, *Colossians*, 56).

the God and Father of our Lord Jesus Christ always when "praying for you" (1:3), thus reinforcing the loving care and concern that closely unites Paul and Timothy with their audience.

Paul and Timothy pray that the audience's experiential knowledge of the grace of God in truth (1:6) progresses to their being filled by God (divine passive) with the knowledge of God's will in all wisdom and the understanding that comes from the Spirit (1:9).[17] The audience are faithful brothers (and sisters) within the realm of being "in Christ" (1:2). They have come to know the grace of God within the realm of being "in truth" (1:6) established by the truth of the gospel (1:5). And they have love within the realm of being "in the Spirit" (1:8). Paul and Timothy thus pray that they may now progress to being filled with the knowledge of God's will within the realm of being "in all wisdom and Spiritual understanding" (1:9b).[18]

The purpose of the prayer is that the hearers "walk worthy of the Lord for every desire to please, in every good work bearing fruit and growing with regard to the knowledge of God" (1:10).[19] This further develops the statement that "as indeed in all the world it is bearing fruit and growing, so also among you, from the day you heard and came to know the grace of God in truth" (1:6). As the gospel *in all* the world is *bearing fruit and growing*, from the time the audience *came to know* the grace of *God* in truth, so, the prayer is, *in every* good work the audience may be *bearing fruit and growing* with regard to the *knowledge* of *God*.[20] Regarding the theme of knowledge, the prayer is that the audience, who "have come to know" the grace of God in truth (1:6), may be filled by God with the "knowledge" of God's will (1:9b), so that they may bear

---

17. "The motif of 'fullness' recurs frequently in this epistle (note the different terms used at 1:19, 24, 25; 2:2, 3, 9, 10; 4:12, 17)" (O'Brien, *Colossians*, 20).

18. "[T]he combination of 'wisdom and understanding' is a repeated feature of Jewish writings. Here, too, the wisdom in particular is understood as given through the law, but it is equally recognized that such wisdom can come only from above (as in Wis 9:9–10). And particularly to be noted is the recognition that wisdom and understanding come only from the Spirit" (Dunn, *Colossians*, 70–71).

19. "Paul often characterizes the life and behavior of the Christian by this verb 'walk' and in this he is indebted to the OT. . . . There is no doubt that in the context of this intercessory prayer, and in the light of the apostle's use of the cognate verb, *areskeia* [desire to please] refers to pleasing the Lord" (O'Brien, *Colossians*, 22–23).

20. On 1:10 Dunn (*Colossians*, 72) states, "The imagery of 'bearing fruit and increasing' echoes 1:6, but this time clearly in reference to moral maturity."

fruit and grow with regard to the "knowledge" of God, as their ethical worship by which they may please God (1:10).

As the prayer continues, the audience are to be empowered "in all power according to the might of his glory for all endurance and patience" (1:11). The prayer is thus that the audience may be gifted and equipped by God in a comprehensive way, so that they are not lacking in anything they may need with regard to their conduct and way of life, their ethical worship of pleasing God.[21] And it alerts the audience to their need for all endurance and patience in the face of possible opposition regarding alternative claims of how they should worship God.[22]

Previously Paul and Timothy expressed their worship of "thanking" God as the Father in regard to the Colossians' love for all other believers—all the holy ones (1:3–4). They now pray that the Colossians themselves join in this worship by joyfully "thanking" the Father, who has made them fit for the share of the inheritance together with all other believers—the holy ones in the light (1:12). Paul and Timothy's prayer, then, is for their audience to be joyfully thanking God the Father for having made them, as composed mainly of Gentiles, fit or worthy for the share of the inheritance originally meant for the chosen people of Israel. It is now destined for all the holy ones as the new people of God, believing Jews and Gentiles alike.

Worship in the Body of the Letter

That God has now reconciled the Colossians in the body of the sacrificial "flesh" of Christ through his death (1:22) complements God's having made peace with the entire cosmos through the sacrificial "blood" of the cross of Christ (1:20). The consequence is that God might present the Colossians, who, as Gentiles formerly involved in idolatrous worship, were once alienated from and enemies of God, as now holy and

21. "In all power" in 1:11 "implies all the spiritual resources necessary to their Christian life," according to Wilson (*Colossians*, 108).

22. On "all endurance and patience" Dunn (*Colossians*, 74) comments, "The two nouns are near synonyms. Both are included not so much because of their distinctive meanings but to reinforce the point that hope of heavenly glory in the future requires patience and endurance now (not least in the face of alternative religious claims) and that both the present patience and the future transformation are the outworking of the same glorious might."

unblemished and blameless before Christ. That God might present the audience as "holy" and "unblemished" and "blameless" before Christ (1:22) functions as a rhetorical triplet within a combination of cultic and juridical imagery. "Presenting" someone "before" Christ means presenting one as an acceptable sacrificial offering for approval before Christ, as well as presenting one deemed to be completely innocent and worthy before the judgment of Christ.[23]

This rhetorically rich combination impresses upon the audience, first of all, in accord with the cultic side of the imagery, that the sacrificial offering of Christ through his death on the cross has graciously transformed them likewise into a sacrificial offering—indeed, one that is "holy and unblemished and blameless" and thus serves as pleasing worship before Christ himself. Secondly, in accord with the juridical side of the imagery, the audience are to realize that the sacrificial death of Christ has empowered them to live as morally "holy" and "unblemished" and "blameless" ones both now and for the final judgment before Christ. This means that, as those whom God has reconciled and with whom God has made peace through Christ, the audience need no longer conduct themselves in works that are evil (1:21), which do not render proper ethical worship to God. They now can and must behave as those whom God, both now and ultimately, is to present as "holy and unblemished and blameless" before Christ (1:22). They will complete this pleasing ethical worship "if indeed you persevere in the faith, having been established and steadfast and not shifting from the hope of the gospel which you heard, which was proclaimed in all creation that is under heaven, of which I became, I, Paul, a minister" (1:23).[24]

23. "Cultic terminology is employed in this statement. So the words 'holy' and 'blameless' are used to describe the unblemished animals set apart for God as OT sacrifices" (O'Brien, *Colossians*, 68). "The imagery is drawn from cult and law court and reflects the degree to which these two powerful features of daily life in classical society were interwoven. *Paristēmi* ('present') here signifies a formal bringing before and presentation in the implied hope of acceptance and acknowledgment. Thus it could be used both of offering a sacrifice and of bringing someone before a judge" (Dunn, *Colossians*, 109).

24. "There is implicit, then, an interplay between the idea of Christ's death as sacrifice (1:20) and the presentation of those who are as unblemished as a sacrifice to God. In other words, there is an echo of the Pauline idea of sacrificial interchange, where the spotless sacrifice by dying as a sin offering is somehow interchanged with the blameworthy sinner and its spotlessness transferred to the sinner. This has been taken up in the imagery of formal presentation to judge or king or emperor, where it

Paul and Timothy informed the audience previously that they do not cease praying that God may fill them with the knowledge of God's will in all the wisdom and understanding that comes from the Spirit, to "walk," that is, to conduct their lives and behave in their ethical worship, as worthy of the Lord for every desire to please, in every good work bearing fruit and growing with regard to the knowledge of God (1:9–10). Now Paul exhorts his audience that, as they have received the Christ, Jesus the Lord, in him, they are to "go on walking" in their ethical worship, as those who have been rooted and are being built up in him (2:6–7). And that the audience are to be abounding within the realm of "thanksgiving" (2:7) reinforces how they are with joy to be "thanking" the Father who has made them fit for the share of the inheritance of the holy ones in the light (1:12). Their grateful worship is thus to follow the lead of Paul and Timothy, who are "thanking" God the Father of our Lord Jesus Christ always when praying for their Colossian audience (1:3).[25]

The metaphorical or spiritual "circumcision" with which the audience were "circumcised" as a ritual of initiation happened "in the removal of the body of the flesh" (2:11), recalling for the audience that God has now reconciled them in the "body" of the "flesh" of Christ through his sacrificial death (1:22). The audience are to infer that by this reconciliation that God accomplished for them through the body of the flesh of Christ in his sacrificial death, they have had their own body of the flesh metaphorically "removed," so that they are now part of the "body," which is the church (1:18, 24), and of which Christ is the head (1:18). This is confirmed for the audience as "in the removal of the body of the flesh" is further explained as "in the circumcision of the

---

is the irreproachable character of those presented that guarantees their acceptance. But it is clearly implicit that this acceptability has been made possible and guaranteed by the death of Christ" (Dunn, *Colossians*, 109–10). "Paul emphasizes that Christ has accomplished this perfection for us, it does not come from our own striving. But God's goal of making us a holy and blameless people in Christ is still a work in progress, and it requires some response on our part. Christians need to recognize that they have been reconciled to God to live a life that God approves" (Garland, *Colossians*, 97).

25. "[T]he implication is that a characteristic and fundamental feature of their relation with Jesus as Christ and Lord should be gratitude for what God has done in and through him. As rootedness and foundation depends on the faith called forth by the gospel, so growing from the root and building up on the foundation can be successful only in an atmosphere of thankfulness to God" (Dunn, *Colossians*, 143).

Christ" (2:11). This spiritual "circumcision" not made with hands, taking place in the "removal" of the body of the flesh, is the "circumcision" God accomplished for the audience in and through the sacrificial death of the Christ, whom the audience have received (2:6), but with whom the "philosophy of empty deceit" is not in accord (2:8).[26]

The audience then hear their spiritual "circumcision" (2:11) further delineated as their "having been buried with" Christ metaphorically "in the baptism" (2:12), that is, in their immersion or washing in water as the initiation ritual they underwent when they became Christians. It is in and through their baptism then that the audience have experienced the "removal" of the body of the flesh, and thus the "circumcision" of the Christ, by which they became part of the body of Christ, the church. Their having been "buried with" Christ in their baptism is thus part of their having received the Christ (2:6) and appropriated the reconciliation God accomplished for them in the body of the flesh of Christ through his sacrificial death (1:22). That death implicitly includes a burial that the audience have undergone metaphorically, spiritually, and ritually with Christ in their baptism. Not only have the audience been "buried with" Christ in their baptism, but "in him indeed you were raised with him through faith in the working of the God who raised him from the dead" (2:12).[27]

---

26. "v. 11 presents spiritual circumcision, not baptism, as the Christian counterpart to physical circumcision. A contrast is implied between circumcision as an external, physical act performed by human hands on a portion of the flesh eight days after birth and circumcision as an inward, spiritual act carried out by divine agency on the whole fleshly nature at the time of regeneration. Although the OT knew of such a 'circumcision of the heart' (Deut. 10:16, 30:6; Jer. 4:4; Ezek. 44:7), Paul speaks of this divestiture of the old man as distinctively 'Christ's circumcision,' a circumcision that characterizes the followers of Christ" (Harris, *Colossians*, 103). "Christians have already received the true circumcision in the putting off of the body of flesh in the circumcision of Christ. No further ascetic practice, as a means of putting off fleshly desires, can enhance this. There is therefore a further reminder here of the sufficiency of Christ" (Smith, *Heavenly Perspective*, 96).

27. "The imagery is forceful, of sinking below the waters of baptism as a kind of burial. Baptism, presumably by immersion, represented mimetically the commitment to enter the tomb with Jesus after he has been taken down from the cross. Since burial was understood as the conclusion of the event of dying, this commitment meant the enacted willingness to identify oneself with the complete event of Jesus' death. The passive tense indicates also the yielding of those being baptized to the baptizer as indicative of their surrender to God" (Dunn, *Colossians*, 159).

Recalling his previous warning, "See to it that there will not be anyone who is captivating you through the philosophy which is empty deceit" (2:8), Paul elaborates upon it: "Let then no one judge you in food and in drink or in regard to a festival or new moon or sabbaths" (2:16). The audience must take heed lest any advocate of the "philosophy of empty deceit," with its association to the teachings and practices of the Jewish synagogue, "judge," that is, criticize, find fault with, or even condemn them for not adhering to some of the ways of Jewish worship. These include Jewish regulations regarding what not to eat and drink, as well as the observance of Jewish days of worship—the annual festivals, or monthly (new moon) celebrations, or weekly periods of rest and worship in the synagogue on the sabbath.[28]

While these Jewish practices and observances are a "shadow," that is, a forerunner or anticipation, of the things that were to come, the "body" belongs to the Christ (2:17). For the audience the phrase "the body belongs to the Christ" carries a double meaning. That the "body" belongs to the Christ means that the substance or reality of the things to come, which the previously mentioned Jewish practices and observances only anticipate or foreshadow, have already become a reality in Christ. At the same time, that the "body" belongs to the Christ means that the audience, as part of the "body" which is the church, belong to the Christ as the head who both rules over and sustains the body (1:18, 24). The audience are to realize, then, that as part of the "body" they have been and are being filled with all the fullness of the deity in their union with Christ, the head, in whom all the fullness of the deity dwells in a "bodily" manner (2:9–10). They have already begun to enjoy the reality (the "body") of "the things that were to come," to which these Jewish practices of worship, as a "shadow," are still looking forward. They therefore need not engage in such worship.

One who would condemn for not observing the practices of Jewish worship is caricatured as one "delighting in humility and worship of the angels, going into detail about what things he had seen, vainly being

28. "We must conclude, therefore, that all the elements of this verse bear a characteristically and distinctively Jewish color, that those who cherished them so critically must have been the (or some) Jews of Colossae, and that their criticism arose from Jewish suspicion of Gentiles making what they would regard as unacceptable claims to the distinctive Jewish heritage without taking on all that was most distinctive of that heritage" (ibid., 175).

made arrogant by the mind of his flesh" (2:18). This description serves as a polemical parody of the kind of conduct practiced by one proudly engaging in the experience of a type of Jewish mystical or ecstatic visions of heavenly worship. "Delighting in humility" parodies the taking of pleasure in the kind of humility that involves fasting as an inducement to ecstatic, mystical, visionary experiences. That the one who would condemn the audience delights also "in worship of the angels" further parodies these visions of heavenly worship. Although one delighting in this kind of visionary worship stimulated by the "humility" of fasting may highly esteem it as a participation in the angelic worship of God in heaven, the audience are to devalue it as an obsessive and idolatrous worship of merely the angels themselves rather than authentic worship of God.[29]

"Going into detail about what he has seen" (2:18) seems to confirm that this sort of "worship" involves visionary experiences—indeed, visions of heavenly worship that one proudly delights in delineating to others in detail. But the audience are to consider such a person who would condemn them for not engaging in this kind of visionary worship as "vainly being made arrogant by the mind of his flesh" (2:18). Such worship cannot be seen as involving true humility or amounting to anything significant, since it ironically leads to "vainly being made arrogant." The visions involved in such worship, alleged to be seen in heaven, actually take place nowhere but in "the mind of his flesh."[30] The

29. According to Dunn (*Colossians*, 180–81), there "is the evidence of a desire particularly within apocalyptic and mystical circles of first-century Judaism to join in with the worship of angels in heaven. . . . It is quite possible, therefore, to envisage a Jewish (or Christian Jewish) synagogue in Colossae which was influenced by such ideas and which delighted in their worship sabbath by sabbath as a participation in the worship of the angels in heaven. In this case the 'humility' associated with this worship could very well denote the spiritual discipline and mortification regarded as essential to maintain the holiness required to participate with the holy ones and the holy angels." "In the polemical context that expresses Paul's contempt for the arrogance of the 'philosophy,' the reference to 'the worship of angels' may well be a biased description of its practices. If the errorists were actually and actively worshiping angels, we would expect Paul to spew forth a far more passionate denunciation of such idolatry. We may infer from his relative calm on the issue that they are not actually offering worship to angelic beings or invoking them. Thus, Paul may only be disdainfully caricaturing the 'philosophy's' ritual concerns and attention to New Moons as the worship of angels" (Garland, *Colossians*, 179).

30. "To speak of 'the mind of flesh' was therefore in effect to deny that this

audience are thus to shun such "worship" that leads to one being made arrogant in his "flesh," since they, who were once spiritually "dead" in the "uncircumcision" of their "flesh" (2:13), have had the body of their "flesh" removed by God in the "circumcision" of the Christ (2:11), so that they are now part of the body, the church, of which Christ is the head (1:18, 24).

Unlike the audience, such a condemnatory, proud, and vainly arrogant person preoccupied with a merely fleshly way of thinking amounting to a very individualistic kind of "worship" is consequently "not holding to the head, from whom the whole body, supported and held together through ligaments and bonds, grows with the growth that is from God" (2:19). The audience are to realize and appreciate that they, who have received the Christ (2:6), are thus holding to the Christ who is the "head," the authoritative "head" superior to every angelic principality and authority (2:10), so that they need not engage in any type of individualistic, visionary "worship" of the angels. Instead, the audience are to hold to the Christ as the "head" from whom the whole "body," the "body" that is the church of which Christ is the "head" (1:18), the "body" that belongs to Christ (2:17), is supported and held together through its individual members, metaphorically described as its "ligaments and bonds." It grows, not individualistically but corporately, with the growth that is authentically from God and by which they may offer worship pleasing to God.[31]

That the audience are addressed as God's chosen ones who are also "holy ones" reminds them that the new moral behavior they are enjoined to "put on" (3:12) is appropriate to their status among God's "holy ones" to whom the mystery of God, Christ (2:2), has been manifested (1:26). It correlates to their status as those whom God reconciled through the death of Christ to present them as "holy ones" without any

---

Colossian worshiper with angels could ever have 'lifted off' from earth: even his mind was 'flesh,' fast bound to earth" (Dunn, *Colossians*, 185). "For Paul, the mind of the flesh is something set over against God and lacks any true spiritual enlightenment" (Garland, *Colossians*, 181). "The irony of this passage shows that boasting of 'heavenly' visions was, in fact, worldly" (Smith, *Heavenly Perspective*, 131).

31. "Paul is therefore appealing to the sufficiency of Christ who is the source of nourishment for the body. This growth of the church is dependent on a correct understanding of the person of Christ, not on ecstatic heavenly ascents. The individual Christian is to be more concerned for the unity of the body than for boasting in heavenly experiences" (Smith, *Heavenly Perspective*, 132).

moral blemish or blame before Christ (1:22). The audience were commanded to "put to death" the parts that are upon the earth (3:5) and to
"put away" their old immoral behavior toward one another, exemplified
by a list of five vices—anger, rage, malice, slander, obscene talk from
your mouth (3:8). So, correlatively, they are commanded to "put on"
a new moral behavior toward one another, exemplified by a list of five
virtues—heartfelt compassion, kindness, humility, gentleness, patience
(3:12). This list of virtues exemplifies the new type of moral "clothing"
that, as part of their ethical worship, the audience are to "put on" in
relating to one another regardless of their ethnic-religious or sociocultural status (3:11) now that they have "removed" the "old human
being" (3:9) and "put on" the "new human being" (3:10).[32]

In contrast to the false "humility" of the deceitful philosophy (2:8)
that delights in "humility" and worship of angels (2:18) and that has a
reputation of wisdom in self-chosen worship and "humility" and severe treatment of the body, but is not of any value to anyone (2:23),
the audience is to "put on" an authentic "humility," the central term in
the fivefold list of virtues (3:12). That the audience are to "put on" the
virtue of "patience" as the final, climactic virtue in the fivefold list (3:12)
reminds them of the authors' prayer that they be empowered by God
for all endurance and "patience" (1:11) to "walk," that is, conduct themselves and behave, as their ethical worship worthy of the Lord (1:10).[33]

Paul then indicates how the ethical and liturgical worship of the
Colossians is interrelated. As he prayerfully declares, "And let the peace
of Christ rule in your hearts, to which indeed you were called in one
body. And be thankful. Let the word of Christ dwell in you richly, in
all wisdom teaching and admonishing each other with psalms, hymns,
and Spiritual songs, in grace singing in your hearts to God" (3:15–16).[34]
As an appropriate response to being called by God in one body (3:15b)

32. "Paul is enjoining the Colossians to wear those moral garments that are appropriate to their calling and status" (Harris, *Colossians*, 160).

33. "Paul earlier (1:11) prayed that this sort of character would appear in the
Colossians; he now urges them to make his prayer come true" (Wright, *Colossians*, 142).

34. For this construal and punctuation of 3:16 in which a comma is placed after
rather than before "psalms, hymns, and Spiritual songs", see Fee (*God's Empowering
Presence*, 653), who adds that this "view results in a (typically Pauline) nicely balanced
set of ideas, each of which expresses the twin dimensions of Christian worship—hori-
zontal and vertical—with the various kinds of songs as the 'swing component' that
conceptually ties the two parts together."

to the peace of Christ, which is to rule in their hearts (3:15a), so that they may be at peace with God and one another in that one body, the audience are exhorted to the worship of being "thankful" to God (3:15c). This recalls and reinforces how they are to be abounding in "thanksgiving" to God who "rooted" and "built" them up in Christ and confirmed them in the faith (2:7). It also recalls and reinforces how they are to be "thanking" the Father, who has made them fit for the share of the inheritance of the holy ones in the light (1:12). And it more closely associates them with the authors, Paul and Timothy, who "thank" the God and Father of our Lord Jesus Christ always when praying for the audience (1:3).

That the audience are to let the word of Christ dwell in them richly (3:16a), especially as they hear it proclaimed in their liturgical worship, means they are to appropriate within them all the richness of understanding, knowledge, and wisdom associated with the mystery of Christ. The audience have already been informed of the authors' continual praying that they may be filled with the knowledge of God's will "in all wisdom" and Spiritual understanding (1:9). As they pro-claim Christ, the authors are "admonishing" every human being and "teaching" every human being "in all wisdom," that they may present every human being complete in Christ (1:28). And now the Colossian audience are to be part of this ministry. As a result of their allowing the word of Christ to dwell in them richly, appropriating all the rich-ness of understanding, knowledge, and wisdom that comes from the mystery of Christ, they are enabled "in all wisdom" to be "teaching" and "admonishing" each other as their ethical worship in and through their liturgical worship—with psalms, hymns, and Spiritual songs (3:16b).[35]

The audience may actualize their being thankful to God (3:15c) in their corporate worship in the one body (3:15b) by gratefully singing "in grace" (3:16c), that is, within the realm of the "grace" of God the authors have prayed for them (1:2), the "grace" of God in truth they came to know (1:6), as they learned the gospel from Epaphras (1:7).[36]

35. Thus, "singing can be both 'to God' and a means of 'teaching one another,'" as pointed out by Fee (*God's Empowering Presence*, 652): "Such songs are at the same time creedal, full of theological grist and give evidence of what the early Christians most truly believed about God and his Christ" (ibid., 656).

36. With reference to the meaning of the attitude of being "in grace" in 3:16, Fee (*God's Empowering Presence*, 655) states, "the focus is not so much on *our* attitude to-

In this grace they are to be singing with psalms, hymns, and Spiritual songs (3:16c)—a rhetorical triplet of synonymous terms climaxing with a more elaborate third term, "Spiritual" songs, that is, songs appropriate to their being within the realm of the divine "Spirit" (1:8; cf. 2:5) of God, echoing the "Spiritual" understanding with which they are to be filled by God (1:9).[37] They are to be singing these songs not only externally with their mouths but internally "in your hearts" to God (3:16c),[38] just as they are to let the peace of Christ dwell internally "in your hearts" (3:15a). They are thus to be singing in their hearts to "God" as an appropriate response to their being chosen ones of "God" (3:12).[39] Indeed, in every word that the audience speak and in every work that they do in both their liturgical and ethical worship, they are to do everything in the name of their Lord Jesus, gratefully thanking God the Father through that same Lord, the Christ whom they have received and in union with whom they are to conduct all aspects of their lives (3:17; 2:6).

Worship in the Letter's Closing

As the letter begins to come to a close, the Colossian audience are exhorted regarding their worship of praying to and thanking God. At the beginning of the letter the audience heard how the praying of the authors for them was closely combined with their thanksgiving to God: "We thank God the Father of our Lord Jesus Christ always when pray-

---

ward God as we sing, but on our awareness of *his* toward us that prompts such singing in the first place" (emphases original). "[T]he response of praise depends as much on God's grace as their initial reception of the gospel" (Dunn, *Colossians*, 239).

37. "We are dealing with songs that are inspired by the Spirit" (Fee, *God's Empowering Presence*, 653).

38. The sense is "'singing with your whole heart,'" according to Fee (ibid., 655). "As in 3:15 the addition of 'in (or with) your hearts' underlines the importance of a worship rooted in the depths of personal experience and springing up from that source—heart worship and not merely lip worship" (Dunn, *Colossians*, 239–40).

39. "It is thus consistent that Paul should conclude this issue of reconciliation by referring to worship in 3.16–17. This has direct relevance to the Colossian error, where the adherents of the philosophy were belittling the worship of the Colossian Christians by claiming a higher heavenly worship with the angels (2.18). In this context, Paul implies that the worship of the Colossian Christians should be sufficient" (Smith, *Heavenly Perspective*, 201).

ing for you" (1:3). The audience was assured of the authors' perseverance in this regard, as they repeat: "We do not cease praying on behalf of you" (1:9). The audience are likewise to be "thanking the Father" (1:12), "abounding in thanksgiving" (2:7), "be thankful" (3:15), and "thanking God the Father through him (Christ)" (3:17). And now, just as the authors do not cease in praying for the audience when they thank God, so the audience are to "persevere in prayer, being watchful in it in thanksgiving" (4:2).[40] They are to be "praying" not only for themselves but at the same time, in reciprocation of the authors' praying for them, "for us"—Paul and Timothy (4:3a; cf. 1:1–2). They are to pray specifically that God may open for Paul and Timothy a door for the word of the gospel about Christ, that it may be heard and received by others as it was by the Colossian believers (4:3b).

The Colossians are assured that Epaphras is "always" struggling "on behalf of you" in the "prayers" (4:12). This strengthens his similarity to Paul and Timothy, who are "always praying" for the audience (1:3), indeed, who do not cease "praying on behalf of you"(1:9). These similarities make the audience aware of the continuing concern of Epaphras, from whom they learned the word of the truth of the gospel (1:5–7), as he struggles and prays for them. They add weight to the authority of Paul (and Timothy), further prompting the audience to fulfill the letter's expectations of them.

At the beginning of the letter the audience were addressed by both Paul and Timothy (1:1). But eventually they were addressed solely by Paul with great emphasis upon his own person, as they heard him tell them not to shift from the hope of the gospel, of which "I became, I, Paul, a minister" (1:23). The audience were then informed, with more emphasis upon the person of Paul, that he is suffering on behalf of them and on behalf of the whole church, of which "I became, I, a minister" (1:25). And now the audience hear, again with great emphasis upon the person of Paul, of the greeting "in my own hand, of Paul" (4:18a).[41]

---

40. "The other accompanying exhortation is once again that their prayers should be made in a spirit of thanksgiving (*en eucharistia*). This repeated emphasis in Colossians makes it one of the most 'thankful' documents in the New Testament (1:3, 12; 2:7; 3:17; 4:2)" (Dunn, *Colossians*, 262).

41. "Having finished dictating, Paul takes up his pen to add a personal greeting in his own handwriting. The apostle always concluded his letters autobiographically even where there is no explicit acknowledgment of it. His personal signatures occur

The first part of Paul's final greeting, the exhortation to keep on re-membering my "chains" or "bonds" (4:18b), reinforces for the audience Paul's assertion that it is on account of the mystery of the Christ that "I have been bound" (4:3d). This "binding" carries a double nuance. Paul is "bound" literally and physically in prison, and Paul is "bound" metaphorically and spiritually on account of his speaking the mystery of the Christ. Thus, Paul's exhortation to the audience to remember my "chains" not only serves as a final reminder to them of Paul's literal and physical suffering in prison on their behalf and on behalf of the whole church (1:24–25), but reminds them to pray (4:2–3b) that he may manifest the mystery of the Christ as it is necessary, as he is "bound," to speak it (4:3c–4).[42]

The second part of Paul's greeting, which concludes the letter, "the grace with you" (4:18c), brings to a climax the audience's involvement in the grace that comes from God. It reinforces Paul and Timothy's prayer-ful greeting at the beginning of the letter of "grace" to you and peace from God our Father (1:2c).[43] It prays for a continuation in the "grace" of God in truth, which the audience have already come to know (1:6), so that they are not captivated by the false "philosophy" of empty deceit (2:8). It complements the exhortation for the audience to "let the word of Christ dwell in you richly, in all wisdom teaching and admonishing

frequently (1 Cor 16:21; 2 Cor 10:1; Gal 6:11; Col 4:18; 2 Thess 3:17 and Philem 19) and were a common epistolary technique in the first century" (O'Brien, *Colossians*, 259). "At all events it reinforces the effect of the letter in providing a real substitute for the personal presence of the one absent" (Dunn, *Colossians*, 289).

42. "It is possible that Paul is here requesting continued intercession for himself. The sense would then be, 'Keep remembering before God in prayer my imprisonment for the gospel' (cf. 4:3–4)" (Harris, *Colossians*, 215–16). "Again the brevity and the failure to follow Paul's normal practice of citing the title of Christ with its liturgical resonance strongly suggest that the words here were penned under considerable diffi-culty, so that only the most basic benediction could be given" (Dunn, *Colossians*, 290). "The call to remember his chains is not some forlorn plea for pity from a woebegone and disheartened apostle. He does not ask for commiseration. He is glad to suffer for Christ (1:24) and his bonds are the bonds of the gospel (Philem. 13). It is better to regard this call as a note of encouragement for those who may also suffer persecution for their faith as well as another request for their prayer support" (Garland, *Colossians*, 282).

43. "The final benediction picks up the introductory greeting (1:2) where Paul desires that the Colossians may apprehend more fully the grace of God in which they stand. At the same time the note of confidence is also struck. God's grace will sustain the community, for it is by grace alone that they will stand" (O'Brien, *Colossians*, 260).

each other with psalms, hymns, and Spiritual songs, in grace singing in your hearts to God" (3:16). And it complements the exhortation for the audience to "let your word always be in grace, seasoned with salt, to know how it is necessary for you to answer each one" (4:6).[44]

Conclusion: Worship in Colossians

As the letter begins, Paul's greeting of God's "grace" to "you," his Colossian audience, expresses his prayer that God, who has already graced the audience in making them holy ones and believers in Christ, will grant them yet further divine grace, during and as a result of their listening to the letter itself (1:2). The prayer report that Paul and Timothy thank the God and Father of our Lord Jesus Christ "always when praying for *you*" (1:3) reinforces the opening greeting and prayer that "grace and peace from God our Father be with *you*" (1:2). Paul and Timothy pray that the audience may be gifted and equipped by God in a comprehensive way, so that they are not lacking in anything they may need with regard to their conduct and way of life, their ethical worship of pleasing God (1:9–11). They pray that the Colossians join in their thanksgiving worship by joyfully thanking God the Father for having made them, as composed mainly of Gentiles, fit or worthy for the share of the inheritance originally meant for the chosen people of Israel (1:12).

As those whom God has reconciled and with whom God has made peace through Christ, the Colossians need no longer conduct themselves in works that are evil (1:21), which do not render proper ethical worship to God. They now can and must behave as those whom God, both now and ultimately, is to present as a "sacrificial" worship that is "holy and unblemished and blameless" before Christ (1:22). They will complete this pleasing ethical worship "if indeed you persevere in the faith, having been established and steadfast and not shifting from the hope of the gospel which you heard, which was proclaimed in all

44. "From one point of view, grace has been the subject of the whole letter. Paul has written in order to emphasize the undeserved love of God in Christ, and all that follows from it. From another point of view, grace has been the *object* of the letter: Paul has written in order to be a *means* of grace, not merely to describe it. The letter closes as it began, in grateful prayer" (Wright, *Colossians*, 162, emphasis original).

creation that is under heaven, of which I became, I, Paul, a minister" (1:23). As they have received the Christ, Jesus the Lord, in him, the Colossians are to "go on walking" in their ethical worship, as those who have been rooted and are being built up in him, abounding within the realm of "thanksgiving" to God (2:6–7).

The sacrificial death of Christ implicitly includes a burial that the Colossians have undergone metaphorically, spiritually, and ritually with Christ in their baptism. Not only have the audience been "buried with" Christ in their baptism, but "in him indeed you were raised with him through faith in the working of the God who raised him from the dead" (2:12).

The Colossians are to realize and appreciate that they, who have received the Christ (2:6), are thus holding to the Christ who is the "head," the authoritative "head" superior to every angelic principality and authority (2:10). They need not engage in any type of individualistic, visionary "worship" of the angels advocated by a Jewish "philosophy of empty deceit" (2:8). Instead, they are to hold to the Christ as the "head" from whom the whole "body"—the "body" that is the church of which Christ is the "head" (1:18), the "body" that belongs to Christ (2:17)—is supported and held together through its individual members, metaphorically described as its "ligaments and bonds" (2:19). It grows not individualistically but corporately, with the growth that is authentically from God and by which they may offer worship pleasing to God.

In contrast to the false "humility" of the deceitful philosophy (2:8) that delights in "humility" and worship of angels (2:18) and that has a reputation of wisdom in self-chosen worship and "humility" and severe treatment of the body, but is not of any value to anyone (2:23), the Colossians are to "put on" an authentic "humility" (3:12). That they are also to "put on" the virtue of "patience" (3:12) reminds them of the authors' prayer that they be empowered by God for all endurance and "patience" (1:11) to "walk," that is, conduct themselves and behave, as their ethical worship worthy of the Lord (1:10).

The Colossians are to allow the word of Christ to dwell in them richly (3:16a), appropriating all the richness of understanding, knowledge, and wisdom that comes from the mystery of Christ (1:9). They are thereby enabled in all wisdom to be teaching and admonishing each other as their ethical worship in and through their liturgical worship—

with psalms, hymns, and Spiritual songs (3:16b). In every word that they speak and in every work that they do in both their liturgical and ethical worship, they are to do everything in the name of their Lord Jesus, gratefully thanking God the Father through that same Lord, the Christ, whom they have received and in union with whom they are to conduct all aspects of their lives (3:17; 2:6).

The Colossians are to "persevere in prayer, being watchful in it in thanksgiving" (4:2). They are to be "praying" not only for themselves but at the same time, in reciprocation of the authors' praying for them, "for us"—Paul and Timothy (4:3a; cf. 1:1–2). They are to pray specifically that God may open for Paul and Timothy a door for the word of the gospel about Christ, that it may be heard and received by others as it was by the Colossian believers (4:3b).

Paul's exhortation to the Colossians to remember my "chains" (4:18) not only serves as a final reminder to them of Paul's literal and physical suffering in prison on their behalf and on behalf of the whole church (1:24–25), but reminds them to pray (4:2–3) that he may manifest the mystery of the Christ, as it is necessary, as he is "bound," to speak it (4:3–4). Paul's final greeting, "the grace with you" (4:18), brings to a climax the Colossians' involvement in the grace that comes from God. It reinforces Paul and Timothy's prayerful greeting at the beginning of the letter of "grace" to you and peace from God our Father (1:2), thus placing the entire letter within a framework of worship in response to divine grace. And it prays for a continuation in the "grace" of God in truth, which the Colossians have already come to know (1:6), so that they are not captivated by the false "philosophy" of empty deceit (2:8), with its inauthentic worship.

Ephesians

The words "in Ephesus" are lacking in some early manuscripts containing the letter to the Ephesians, but the best available evidence supports their inclusion.[1] Although it appears to be relevant for and may well have been read to congregations outside of Ephesus, the primary destination of the letter is all of the various local churches within the great Asia Minor metropolis of Ephesus—"the holy ones who are in Ephesus" (Eph 1:1).

Although the letter to the Ephesians presents itself as authored and sent by Paul (1:1; 3:1), many scholars in modern times have questioned and/or denied that the historical apostle Paul could have authored this letter because in their estimation it differs too greatly from the so-called main or undisputed letters of Paul. In their view someone using "Paul" as a pseudonym authored this letter. But recently scholars have pointed out that an appeal to pseudonymity involves problematical assumptions, making it debatable whether any of the letters in the New Testament that present Paul as their primary author are pseudonymous.[2]

Furthermore, recent studies in the role of coauthors, coworkers, and secretaries in the composition of the Pauline letters have indicated the complexity involved in the question of their authorship. Paul may have authored his letters in a broader sense of authorizing or directing their composition in collaboration with fellow workers. The different audiences, situations, and times of composition, could also account for many of the differences among the Pauline letters.[3]

1. Hoehner, *Ephesians*, 140

2. Ellis, *Making of the New Testament*, 324; Wilder, *Pseudonymity*, 265n52; Carson and Moo, *Introduction*, 350.

3. Stirewalt, *Letter Writer*; Gorman, *Apostle of the Crucified Lord*, 477–78; Richards, *First-Century Letter Writing*; Johnson, *Writings*, 240–42.

Along with Philemon, Colossians, Philippians, and 2 Timothy, Ephesians is numbered among the so-called "captivity letters" of Paul, who was in prison when he sent these letters. Rome, Ephesus, and Caesarea have been suggested as possible locations for Paul's imprisonment while authorizing and directing the composition of his captivity letters. Paul spent much time in Ephesus, but there is no evidence that he was ever imprisoned there long enough to compose a letter. The New Testament records imprisonments for Paul in both Caesarea and Rome. Unlike for Philippians and 2 Timothy, the execution of Paul, who was a Roman citizen, does not seem to be an imminent possibility in Philemon, Colossians, and Ephesians. It thus seems more likely that these three letters were sent from his imprisonment at Caesarea rather than Rome. It is plausible that Paul sent Tychicus with all three of these closely related letters from his Caesarean imprisonment. At any rate, that the implied author "Paul" was in prison somewhere for the composition and sending of these letters is significant for their interpretation.[4]

Although addressed primarily to an audience of believers living in the large city of Ephesus, the letter to the Ephesians, while presupposing the general influence of the social and historical environment of the metropolis of Ephesus upon the audience, makes little explicit or specific mention of its Ephesian locale. This can be taken as an indication that Ephesians may be an encyclical letter intended for a more general audience living both in the metropolis of Ephesus and its more distant environs. That wives, husbands, children, parents, slaves, and masters are directly addressed in the "household code" of Ephesians (5:21—6:9) indicates that the various households in which believers gathered for worship would have been the normal setting for the public performance of the letter.

A major concern of Paul in Ephesians is to assure the audience, characterized as "you" who came to believe (1:13) after "we," Paul and all those who first hoped in the Christ (1:12), came to believe, that they are nevertheless united to and incorporated within those who first believed as part of the cosmic unity that is a major theme of the letter. Although the "we" are generally identified as Jewish Christians and the "you" as Gentile Christians, more nuance is needed. It is not a matter of Gentile Christians ("you") being united with Jewish Christians ("we")

---

4. Reicke, *Paul's Letters*, 75, 83; Ellis, *Making of the New Testament*, 266–75.

in general, but of those originating from a Gentile cultural environment and coming to faith more recently, be they Gentiles or Jews, being united with those originating from a Jewish cultural environment and coming to faith earlier, be they Jews or Gentiles.

Although the "we" would be predominantly Christians of a Jewish origin, including Paul, they could include some Gentiles as well, e.g., those like Titus, an early Greek believer who accompanied Paul yet did not become Jewish by being circumcised (Gal 2:1–3). And although the "you" may be predominantly recent Christians of a Gentile origin, they could include those of a Jewish origin who lived in the Diaspora in a Gentile environment without being circumcised, so that they would have been considered "Gentiles" by circumcised Jews (cf. Timothy in Acts 16:1–3, a Christian disciple who was an uncircumcised Jew with a Jewish mother and Greek father, before being circumcised and joining Paul). The "you," then, could include Gentile pagan converts, former Gentile proselytes and "God-fearers," who frequented Jewish synagogues, as well as Diaspora Jews. At any rate, the "you," those who came to believe more recently, are the implied Ephesian audience addressed by Paul as representative of the "we," those who came to believe earlier (Eph 1:12–13; 2:11–22).

Christian love is the theme central to the overall purpose of Ephesians. Throughout the letter the noun "love" occurs ten times (1:4, 15; 2:4; 3:17, 19; 4:2, 15, 16; 5:2; 6:23), the verb "love" also occurs ten times (1:6; 2:4; 5:2, 25[2x]; 28[3x], 33; 6:24), and the adjective "beloved" occurs once (6:21). Within the ten occurrences of the noun "love," of special significance are the six instances of the poignant prepositional phrase "in love" (1:4; 3:17; 4:2, 15, 16; 5:2) to designate the dynamic domain or sphere of love constituted by the complex interaction of God's love for us in Christ empowering both our love for God/Christ and for one another.[5]

---

5. Heil, *Ephesians*.

Ephesians as a Ritual of Worship

Introductory Worship

The letter is sent from "Paul, apostle of Christ Jesus through the will of God, to the holy ones who are in Ephesus, the believers who are in Christ Jesus" (1:1). The audience are to realize that they are able to live as "holy ones," separated from others by God for service to and worship of God, "in" Ephesus because they are believers who are "in" Christ Jesus. They have been incorporated to live in union with Christ Jesus within a new sphere, realm, or domain of existence determined by what God has done in raising Christ Jesus from the dead and exalting him to the heavenly regions.[6]

Paul begins the epistolary worship with a greeting of "grace to you and peace from God our Father and the Lord Jesus Christ" (1:2). With his authority as an apostle of Christ Jesus through the gracious will of God (1:1a), Paul prays that his audience be granted yet further grace (*charis*) as well as the peace that come as gifts from both God our Father and the Lord Jesus Christ. This opening prayer thus prepares the audience for further experiencing and receiving, through their hearing of the letter itself, the divine grace and peace that will empower them to offer ethical worship to God as both the holy ones who are in Ephesus and the believers who are in Christ Jesus (1:1b).[7]

The epistolary worship continues as Paul immediately exclaims, "Blessed the God and Father of our Lord Jesus Christ" (1:3a). In blessing or praising God, Paul is speaking not only for himself but for "us"—his audience and all believers. He thus leads his audience in worship with his exuberant blessing of the God who is not only "our" Father (1:2)

---

6. As "holy ones," the Ephesian audience "are set apart for him [God] and his service; as the people of his own possession they are the elect community of the end time whose lives are to be characterized by godly behaviour," according to O'Brien (*Ephesians*, 87).

7. It is likely that in 1:2 "*charis* is used to refer to all the benefits collectively given through Christ to the elect," according to Whitlark ("Enabling *Charis*," 347). "Paul's readers have already experienced, in some measure, God's grace and peace in the Lord Jesus Christ. The apostle recognizes this, and in his salutation he expresses his desire that these twin blessings may be understood and experienced in greater measure, especially through the letter itself, for these two major themes are taken up again and again throughout Ephesians" (O'Brien, *Ephesians*, 88).

but the Father of "our" Lord Jesus Christ. That Paul and his audience declare God "blessed" (*eulogētos*) most appropriately responds with worship of the God who "blessed (*eulogēsas*) us with every Spiritual blessing (*eulogia*) in the heavenly places in Christ" (1:3b).[8]

These Spiritual blessings empower both liturgical and ethical worship. As a blessing, God chose us in Christ before the foundation of the world that we might be holy and blameless before God in love (1:4). That God chose us that we might be "holy" enables not only the Ephesian audience (1:1) but all believers to be "holy ones," that is, set apart from the world and consecrated for the worship of God. Coupled with "holy" is "blameless" to form an alliterative pair (*hagious kai amōmous*), with an originally cultic background, that now refers to the moral conduct that constitutes ethical worship.[9]

All believers are to be holy and blameless before God within the sphere, realm, or domain of being "in love." This realm includes not only God's love for believers, as indicated by his blessing and choosing them (1:3b–4a), but believers' love for God, as expressed both by their liturgical worship of blessing God (1:3a) and by their ethical worship of living holy and blameless before God by loving one another (1:4b). Indeed, as Paul continues, our being "holy and blameless before him in love" is for the worship of God. It is "to the praise of the glory of his grace with which he graced us in the Beloved" (1:6). That God has already "graced" us believers with his "grace" reinforces Paul's initial prayer that God grant even more of his divine "grace" to the audience (1:2) as a gift of God's love.

The Ephesian audience, the "you" who came to believe after the "we" who first hoped in Christ, have been empowered to love God, Christ, and one another, as those God granted to be in the dynamic

8. "To use the same word for our worship of God and of God's showering us with spiritual gifts is foreign to us, but this double meaning of the word *bless* is common in both the Old and New Testament" (Snodgrass, *Ephesians*, 46). "The generosity of God is prior: it arises from God's own nature as 'one who blesses', to which human beings are bound to respond by blessing him in worship" (Muddiman, *Ephesians*, 66).

9. "The two adjectives *holy and blameless* were used to describe the unblemished animals set apart for God as Old Testament sacrifices. But already within the Old Testament this language was employed to describe ethical purity . . . ethical holiness and freedom from moral blemish" (O'Brien, *Ephesians*, 100–101). "Thus, the bodily obedience of Christians was for Paul the essential expression of worship to God the Creator in the world of everyday" (Lyons, "Holiness in Ephesians," 240).

realm of union with the cosmic Christ, the "head" under whom all things in the universe are on their way to being definitively united (1:10). That the "you" and the "we" believers have been incorporated into this magnificent cosmic unity empowers them to worship God with their lives of love. As Paul repeatedly emphasizes, "in order that we might be to the praise of his glory" (1:12–14).[10]

The epistolary worship of Paul continues as he assures the Ephesians that he does not cease giving thanks to God for them, making mention of them in his prayers (1:15–16), praying that God may grant them the grace of experiencing the great power available to believers united with the risen Christ (1:17–21). God subjected all things under this cosmic Christ and "gave him as head over all things to the church, which is his body, the fullness of the one who is filling all things in all ways" (1:22–23). This grace further motivates the worship of the audience. Within the church as the "body" of Christ, the audience are in a metaphorical "building" that is being fitted together and growing into a "temple holy in the Lord," that is, a temple comprised of "holy ones," both Jewish and Gentile believers, who are united by the love of God for them and their love for one another, "a dwelling place of God in the Spirit" (2:21–22). It is within this "temple" that is "holy" in the Lord as a preeminent place of worship, then, that the audience are to worship God with their lives by being "holy and blameless before him in love" (1:4).[11]

---

10. "The eulogy of vv. 3–14 began with an outburst of praise as Paul blessed God for all the blessings he had showered on his people in the Lord Jesus Christ. The note of praise has been sustained throughout by means of the recurring refrain 'to the praise of his glory' (vv. 6, 12, 14). The recipients of these wide-ranging blessings of salvation, along with Paul, have been stimulated by this recital of God's mighty acts in his Son to express their gratitude and praise" (O'Brien, *Ephesians*, 123).

11. "[T]he traditional Jewish meaning of the 'holy' temple is 'transcoded' and given a new twist as the non-Jews are also allotted a proper place in the temple, that is, 'by the Spirit' . . . the 'Spirit' language here is meant to lay bare the inclusiveness of the new Temple in which Gentiles are integral components. In short, the usefulness of temple symbolism is that it enables the author to transpose the Gentiles from the periphery to the centre of the Jewish symbolic world while sustaining the traditional notion that the 'temple' is still the holy space of God's presence" (Yee, *Jews*, 210–11).

Paul's Magnificent Prayer

The prisoner Paul's tribulations on behalf of "you," his Ephesian audience, is "your" glory (3:13)—a "glory" (*doxa*) that comes from God (1:6, 12, 14, 17, 18) and calls for a response of worship that glorifies God, acknowledging and praising God for his glory. Paul is *the* prisoner, both literally and metaphorically, of Christ Jesus (3:1) and minister of the gospel (3:6–8) "on behalf of you" (3:1, 13)—his Gentile audience of "you" believers. Paul thus bows his knees before the Father in prayer, actualizing in the letter itself the worship he previously reported when he stated that he does not cease giving thanks "for you," making mention of "you" in his prayers (1:16). That Paul dramatically "bows his knees" before the Father (3:14) prepares the audience for a particularly reverential and awe-inspiring prayer on their behalf, involving the cosmic creative and unifying power of God as the Father of all, the Father "from whom every family in heaven and on earth is named" (3:15).[12]

Previously Paul prayed that God, the Father of glory, may give the Ephesians the Spirit so that they may know what is the wealth of the glory of God's inheritance and what is the surpassing greatness of his power for us who believe according to the working of the might of his strength (1:17–19). Now he prays that God the Father may give them according to the wealth of his glory to be strengthened (divine passive) with power through his Spirit in the inner person (3:16). Recalling not only "the wealth of the glory of his inheritance" (1:18) but "according to the wealth of his grace" (1:7; cf. 2:7), that is, the grace with which God graced us in our union with the Beloved as a manifestation of God's glory (1:6), Paul prays that God may give "according to the wealth of his glory" (3:16). This indicates to his audience that Paul is praying for a gift from God that accords with the lavish wealth of the glory God manifested in gracing believers with an abundant wealth of grace as a

---

12. "While hearing the words of 3:14 is not the same as seeing the actual physical act of bowing the knees, the effect of the vivid imagery is impressive. . . . standing was the usual Jewish posture of prayer. Yet surely the function of . . . 3:14 is . . . to persuasively affect the audience members with the emotional image of the author physically bowing in an attitude of worship and entreating God on their behalf. This sort of imagery and entreaty could hardly fail to gain the goodwill and respect of the audience for the author and the message of Ephesians. Since *kamptō* [bow] is the principal verb for the whole sentence, the attitude of respect toward God and its concomitant emotions prevail throughout the prayer and following doxology" (Jeal, *Ephesians*, 113).

gift of the great love with which God loved us (2:4) in our union with Christ. Paul is thus praying that each individual member of his audience interiorly—in the "inner person"—be strengthened with God's power as a gift of God's love given through the agency of God's Spirit.

Paul continues by praying that the Christ may dwell through faith in "your hearts," that is, in your "inner persons," collectively as a community (3:17a). Previously Paul prayed that the "eyes" of "your" collective "heart" may be enlightened through the Spirit, so that you may know the surpassing greatness of the power God worked for us who believe in raising Christ from the dead and seating him at God's right hand in the heavenly places (1:17–19). Now he prays that Christ may dwell through faith in "your hearts" collectively, strengthened with power interiorly as individuals through God's Spirit (3:16).

That Paul's audience already have been and still are "rooted and grounded in love" (3:17b) means not only that they have love for all the holy ones (1:15) and have received love from Paul (3:1–13), but that they have received the great love with which God loved us (2:4) in our union with the Beloved (1:6). That Paul's audience have been "grounded" or "founded" in love reminds them that they have been built upon the "foundation" of the apostles and prophets, Christ Jesus himself being the "capstone" or "head stone" (2:20). And that they have been firmly "planted" or "rooted" in love reminds them that they, who have been built together with believing Jews into a "dwelling place" (2:22) which is a "building" fitted together as a gift of God's love, have been empowered by that love to "grow" into a temple holy in the Lord (2:21), equipped for the worship of God.

Paul continues by praying that they might have the strength to comprehend, along with all the holy ones, "what is the breadth and length and height and depth" (3:18), what is the vast expanse of the cosmic unity of all things being placed under Christ, the head (1:10). The key words here are "with all the holy ones." Isolated individuals cannot comprehend this cosmic unity. It is only as a worshiping community in union with all the holy ones; it is only as united within the church, the body of Christ, the holy temple of the Lord, that believers can comprehend it. Paul prays that this grand comprehension may enable them to "know," that is, to experience, the great and gracious love of Christ that surpasses "knowledge"—all other experiences (3:19a). With this experience of the love of Christ as part of the church, which is the body and the "fullness" of the Christ who is filling all things in all ways (1:23), the audience are being filled by and with the love of Christ. Paul thus prays that they may be filled to all the "fullness" of God (3:19b), that is, to the complete cosmic fullness and unity to which God has destined the church and which the audience may comprehend interiorly as the absolute "breadth and length and height and depth."[13]

This prayer and the first half of the letter reach a rousing climax as Paul leads his Ephesian congregation in an inspiring act of doxological worship: "Now to him who has the power to do far more beyond all that we ask or imagine according to the power that is working in us, to him be glory in the church and in Christ Jesus to all the generations, for ever and ever. Amen!" (3:20–21).[14] Paul's description of God as the one who has the power to do "far more beyond" all that we ask or imagine (3:20a) assures his audience that God can empower them to know the love of Christ that "surpasses" or "goes far beyond" knowledge (3:18). God has the power to do this according to the power that is working in us (3:20b). The power by which God raised Christ from the dead (1:19–20) is the power now working in us through the indwelling of Christ that empowers us to know the love of Christ with a knowledge that far surpasses anything we can ask or imagine.

---

13. "The comprehending subject is the community itself: self-comprehension of the Body. . . . The inner self-comprehension is totally different from a normal comprehension of being as if it stood outside the man who comprehends. This comprehension of the four dimensions is internally related to our self-awareness and to its self-realization (somatization) of the mystery of God in Christ in the community and in all the communities which belong to Christ. . . . The 'you,' for whom the apostle intercedes, are seen standing at the vital 'centre' of the Body. They see it absorbing other groups, new groups of men in the city of Ephesus and in the whole world, elevating them to unity with Christ, the Head who is in heaven. The Body grows and extends in the four dimensions as if it were extending into the whole cosmos and reaching to the infinite fullness of God" (Usami, *Somatic Comprehension*, 177–78).

14. "The final *amēn* acts as a closing liturgical and rhetorical feature. It adds a final note of solemnity and confirmation, possibly uttered as suggestive of a congregational response, thereby encouraging acquiescence and participation in the language of worship that precedes" (Jeal, *Ephesians*, 128). "The 'Amen' makes it clear that the ascription of praise is not simply a matter of the lips, but is the spontaneous response of the whole congregation" (O'Brien, *Ephesians*, 269).

Paul invites his audience to join him in rendering the "glory" (3:21),[15] that is, the praise and honor, that is reciprocally due to God as the one who gives them the power in their inner person according to the wealth of his "glory" (3:16) and who gives them the Spirit of wisdom and revelation to know what is the wealth of his "glory" as the Father of "glory" (1:17–18). They may now appropriately praise God by attributing to God the "glory" in response to the "glory" God gave them as recipients of God's love in their union with Christ as indicated in the rhythmic refrain of the letter's introductory benediction—"to the praise of the glory of his grace with which he graced us in the Beloved" (1:6, 12, 14; cf. 3:13).[16]

Ethical Worship

As "the prisoner in the Lord" (4:1), Paul exhorts the Ephesians to play their part in causing all things to be united under Christ (1:10). By being truthful "in love," believers may cause all things to grow to him, who is the head, the Christ. But each believer, in and through the ethical worship of love, has an important function to perform. It is from Christ that, as Paul asserts, "the whole body, fitted together and held together through every supporting connection according to the working in measure of each individual part, brings about the growth of the body for the building up of itself in love" (4:15–16).[17]

Functioning as a worshiping assembly enables the Ephesians to be filled with the gifts of God's grace within the dynamic realm of be-

15. This is the final and climactic occurrence of the word "glory" in Ephesians.

16. This "doxology sees the Church as the sphere in which God's glory is acknowledged. Glory is ascribed to God in the worship and praise of the redeemed community, but this will be not only in its cultic activity but also in the whole of its existence (cf. 1:6, 12, 14). There is an eschatological aspect to this, for God will only be perfectly glorified in the Church when it fully shares in his glory (cf. 3:13; 5:27)" (Lincoln, *Ephesians*, 217).

17. "If any corporate growth or building up is to take place, love is the indispensable means. . . . Love is the lifeblood of this body, and, therefore, the ultimate criterion for the assessment of the Church's growth will be how far it is characterized by love" (ibid., 264). "If it is only *in love* that the body increases, then it is only *in love* that true Christian ministry will contribute to the building of the body" (O'Brien, *Ephesians*, 316, emphasis original).

ing "in the Spirit" (5:18).[18] Their liturgical worship, their "speaking to each other in psalms and hymns and spiritual songs, singing songs and singing psalms in your hearts to the Lord, giving thanks always and for all things in the name of our Lord Jesus Christ to God the Father" (5:19–20), is to extend to all areas of their lives and become their ethical worship of love. This is indicated grammatically as the participial expressions describing their liturgical worship—speaking in psalms, singing songs, giving thanks—are continued in the immediately following ethical exhortation regarding their mutual love as Christians, "submitting to one another in respect for Christ" (5:21).

This general submission to one another is then further specified: "Wives (submitting) to their own husbands as to the Lord" (5:22). In submitting to their own husbands in respect for Christ (5:21) wives are submitting to the "Lord," that is, to our "Lord" Jesus Christ in whose name the audience are thanking God the Father in their liturgical worship (5:20). In submitting to their husbands, then, the wives in the audience are playing their part in the ethical worship of the community.

That the husband is "head" of the wife as also the Christ is "head" of the church (5:23a) means that as the Christ is not only the authority over but the source of gifts of love for the church, so also the husband is not only the authority over but the source of gifts of love for the wife. That Christ himself is the savior of the body (5:23b), the one who saved the body of believers, the church, as a gift of God's love, reinforces for the audience that Christ as "head" is the source of gifts of love for the church, and thus that the husband as "head" is similarly a source of love for his wife.

As the church submits to Christ in everything, so also wives are to submit to their husbands in "everything" (5:24), echoing "all the things" with which the audience are being filled by Christ (5:18) and for which the audience are "always" thanking God in their communal worship (5:20). For husbands to love their wives as Christ loved the church in a self-sacrificial way (5:25) further illustrates what it means for the audience of believers, as children beloved by God (5:1), to "walk," that is, to conduct their lives, within the realm of being "in love" (5:2a) as part of their ethical worship.[19]

18. Heil, "Ephesians 5:18b," 506–16.

19. "After the exhortation to wives to submit, with its depiction of husbands as

That by his self-sacrificial love Christ might sanctify or make holy the church (5:26a) provides a further basis empowering the church, as the "building" that is being fitted together in union with Christ as the "head stone," to grow into a "temple" holy in the Lord for their worship (2:20–21). This making holy and cleansing from the impurity of a sinful lifestyle is accomplished "by the washing of the water," a reference to the liturgical ritual of baptism, and takes place "in the word" (5:26b), that is, within the dynamic realm established by the proclaimed word of the gospel which empowers those who hear it to believe and be baptized. It was by this "one baptism" (4:5) that the audience were cleansed of the impurity of their sins, reconciled, and united with all other believers in the "one body" of the church for the worship of God.

That the purpose of Christ's self-sacrificial love, twice expressed as his having freely handed himself over (5:2, 25), is that he himself might present to himself the church glorious (5:27a) underlines for the audience how it is the self-sacrificial love of Christ himself that empowers the church to be "glorious." This further develops Paul's climactic doxology that "to God be glory in the church and in Christ Jesus to all generations for ever and ever. Amen!" (3:21). The church made glorious by Christ is thus inspired to worship by giving glory to God.

What it means for the church to be glorious (5:27a) Paul then elaborates for his audience with both negative and positive terms with cultic connotations: "not having a blemish or wrinkle or any such things, but that she might be holy and blameless" (5:27b). That the church might be "holy and blameless" reminds the audience that God chose us believers before the foundation of the world that we might be "holy and blameless" before God in love (1:4). The audience now realize that the self-sacrificial love of Christ, which serves as the motive and model not only for believers to love one another (5:1–2), but also for husbands to

---

heads, what might well have been expected by contemporary readers would be an exhortation to husbands to rule their wives. Instead the exhortation is for husbands to love their wives. . . . Exhortations to husbands to love their wives are found outside the NT, but they are fairly infrequent" (Lincoln, *Ephesians*, 373–74). "This exhortation to husbands to love their wives is unique. It is not found in the OT, rabbinic literature, or in the household codes of the Greco-Roman era. Although the hierarchical model of the home is maintained, it is ameliorated by this revolutionary exhortation that husbands are to love their wives as Christ loved the church" (Hoehner, *Ephesians*, 748).

love their wives (5:25), empowers us believers, the church, to be morally "holy and blameless" in love as our ethical worship.[20]

Worship in the Letter's Closing

In bringing the letter to a close, Paul exhorts the audience to extend love to their fellow believers—all the holy ones—by praying for them through every prayer and petition at every opportunity and in all persistence in the Spirit (6:18). The phrase "for all the holy ones," intensifies the all-embracing, comprehensive nature of the audience's prayer— through "every" prayer at "every" opportunity in "all" persistence for "all" the holy ones. The audience are to pray for *all* the holy ones, including Paul, the very least of "all holy ones" (3:8). In reciprocation for the love Paul demonstrated toward his audience in not ceasing to give thanks for them, making mention of them in his prayers (1:16), so the audience are to demonstrate their love by praying for Paul. They are to pray that speech may be given to him by God, in opening his mouth, in boldness to make known the mystery of the gospel (6:19).[21]

Paul's final greeting for peace to the brothers and love with faith that comes from God the Father and the Lord Jesus Christ (6:23) functions as a prayer for continuing gifts of peace and love from God and Christ. It also indirectly exhorts the audience, who have already received gifts of peace and love through faith in God and Christ to be thus motivated and empowered to extend gifts of peace and love to their fellow believers, in order to be united with them within the dynamic realm of being "in love."

Paul's prayer that peace, *love*, and grace be with all who are *loving* our Lord Jesus Christ in immortality (6:23–24) concludes the letter with

20. "Here, the glory with which the Church as the bride is adorned will be elaborated on in terms of her moral perfection. The bride's beauty is to be all-encompassing and is not to be spoiled by anything, by the least spot or wrinkle. . . . The picture is of Christ preparing a bride for himself that has no physical blemish. But it then becomes crystal clear from the final *hina* clause that this bride's beauty is moral" (Lincoln, *Ephesians*, 377).

21. For the strategic role of prayer in the spiritual warfare believers face against evil powers in Ephesians, see Rosscup, "Prayer in Ephesians," 57–78. "The writer has demonstrated the importance he attaches to prayer, and particularly prayer for awareness of divine power and strengthening through that power, in his own prayers for the readers reported in 1:15–23 and 3:14–21" (Lincoln, *Ephesians*, 452).

a recapitulation that epitomizes how the letter empowers its listeners to walk in love for the unity of all in Christ. The peace, love, and grace that we believers are receiving from God and Christ empower us in turn to share that peace, love, and grace with one another. This is not only to unite us with all believers in the one body of the church (4:1–6), but also that we might cause all things to be united under Christ, the head (4:15–16; 1:10), whom, in response to his love for us, we are loving as the "Beloved" one (1:6) within the dynamic realm of being "in immortality." As the expression of a dynamic realm or sphere, "in immortality," refers to the immortal, risen life both of Christ and those who love him, the life shared now and forever by believers in their union with the risen and exalted Christ in the heavenly places. This means living now and forever in union with the exalted Christ within the dynamic realm of being "in love" (1:4; 3:17; 4:2, 15–16; 5:2).[22]

Conclusion: Worship in Ephesians

After his initial ritualistic greeting of "grace to you and peace from God our Father and the Lord Jesus Christ" (1:2), Paul immediately leads his Ephesian audience in an exuberant act of worship in response to this grace, as he proclaims, "Blessed is the God and Father of our Lord Jesus Christ, who has blessed us in every spiritual blessing in the heavenly places in Christ, as he chose us in him before the foundation of the world that we might be holy and blameless before him in love" (1:3–4). To be "holy and blameless" before God within the dynamic realm of being in God's love means for us to live morally in love of God and one another as our sacrificial worship in response to the great grace of God given to us in Christ. Indeed, our being "holy and blameless before him in love" is for the worship of God, that is, "to the praise of the glory of his grace with which he graced us in the Beloved" (1:6).

The Ephesian audience have been empowered to love God, Christ, and one another, as those God granted to be in the dynamic realm of

22. "Elsewhere the letter has referred to God's love for believers (cf. 2:4) and Christ's love for them (cf. 3:19; 5:2, 25), to believers' love for one another (cf. 1:15; 4:2), to believing husbands' love for their wives (cf. 5:25, 28, 33), and to believers' love in general (cf. 1:4; 3:17; 4:15, 16; 5:2; 6:23), but this is the only place where their love for Christ is made explicit" (Lincoln, *Ephesians*, 466).

union with the cosmic Christ, the "head" under whom all things in the universe are on their way to being definitively united (1:10). That the "you" and the "we" believers have been incorporated into this magnificent cosmic unity empowers them to worship God with their lives of love, as Paul repeatedly emphasizes, "in order that we might be to the praise of his glory" (1:12–14).

Paul assures the Ephesians that he does not cease giving thanks to God for them, praying that God may grant them the grace of experiencing the great power available to believers united with the risen Christ (1:15–21). This grace further motivates the worship of the audience. Within the church as the "body" of Christ, the audience are in a metaphorical "building" that is being fitted together and growing into a "temple holy in the Lord," "a dwelling place of God in the Spirit" (2:21–22). It is within this "temple" that is "holy" in the Lord as a preeminent place of worship, then, that the audience are to worship God with their lives by being "holy and blameless before him in love" (1:4).

The prisoner Paul, bowing his knees before the Father, utters a solemnly profound prayer that, as a "speech act," conveys to his audience an epistolary experience for what he is so ardently praying. Paul prays that they be strengthened with an interior power through God's Spirit, so that, with Christ dwelling through faith in their hearts, rooted and grounded in love, they might have the strength to comprehend, along with all the holy ones, "what is the breadth and length and height and depth," what is the vast expanse of the cosmic unity of all things being placed under Christ, the head. This cosmic unity can be comprehended by them only as a worshiping community in union with all the holy ones; it is only as united within the church, the body of Christ, the holy temple of the Lord, that believers can comprehend it. And it is this grand comprehension that enables them to experience the great and gracious love of Christ that surpasses all other experiences (3:14–19). Paul then climactically concludes this prayer by leading his Ephesian congregation in an inspiring act of doxological worship: "Now to him who has the power to do far more beyond all that we ask or imagine according to the power that is working in us, to him be glory in the church and in Christ Jesus to all the generations, for ever and ever. Amen!" (3:20–21).

Functioning as a worshiping assembly enables the Ephesians to be filled with the gifts of God's grace within the dynamic realm of being "in the Spirit" (5:18). Their liturgical worship, their "speaking to each other in psalms and hymns and spiritual songs, singing songs and singing psalms in your hearts to the Lord, giving thanks always and for all things in the name of our Lord Jesus Christ to God the Father" (5:19–20), is to extend to all areas of their lives and become their ethical worship of love.

The rich theology of marriage that Paul puts forth in Ephesians holds a place of prominence in the ethical worship of love that is to prevail in their households. The marital love of husbands for their wives serves as a microcosm of ethical worship within the macrocosm of the love of Christ for the church. Husbands are to love their wives in the sacrificial manner that Christ loved the church. They thereby play their role in performing the ethical worship enabled by the sacrificial love of Christ. He handed himself over to death in love that he might present to himself the church as a glorious sacrificial victim suitable for the ethical worship of God, that is, "not having a blemish or wrinkle or any of such things, but that she might be holy and blameless" (5:27; cf. 1:4).

The audience are to pray for all the holy ones (6:18), including Paul, that speech may be given to him by God, in opening his mouth, in boldness to make known the mystery of the gospel (6:19). After presenting a concerted theme of love throughout Ephesians, Paul brings this dominant theme to its climactic conclusion, as he closes this epistolary ritual of worship on an exuberant note of love. The final ritualistic greeting functions as a prayer that not only peace and grace but an explicitly emphasized "love" be granted from God the Father and the Lord Jesus Christ not just to his audience but to the "brothers," that is, to all fellow believers who, as an act of ethical worship in response to Christ's gift of eternal life, "love" the Lord Jesus Christ "in immortality" (6:23–24).

Philippians

The letter to the Philippians initially presents itself as authored and sent by both Paul and Timothy (Phil 1:1), but with the occurrence of first-person singular forms after the opening greeting Paul quickly establishes himself as the primary authorial voice—"I thank my God . . . in my every prayer" (1:3–4), etc. Several times it is indicated that the letter was composed and sent while Paul was in "my chains" or "my bonds" (1:7, 13, 14, 17) of imprisonment. But the precise location of his imprisonment is never explicitly stated in the letter. Several possibilities have been proposed: Caesarea, Corinth, Ephesus, Rome. There is no direct literary evidence that Paul was ever imprisoned in Corinth or Ephesus. According to Acts, Paul was imprisoned for a considerable length of time in both Caesarea (Acts 23:23–27:1) and Rome (28:16–31). Since in Philippians Paul has reconciled himself to the distinct possibility of being executed (Phil 1:21–23), and since Rome is the most likely place for Paul as a Roman citizen (Acts 16:37–38; 22:25–29; 23:27) to be executed, Rome, during Paul's imprisonment there as narrated in Acts 28:16–31, probably in 60–62 AD, is the most likely location of his imprisonment for the composition and sending of the letter to the Philippians.[1]

---

1. For fuller discussions of the view that Philippians was composed while Paul was imprisoned in Rome, see O'Brien, *Philippians*, 19–26; Witherington, *Philippians*, 24–26; Fee, *Philippians*, 34–37; Bockmuehl, *Philippians*, 25–32; Cassidy, *Paul in Chains*, 124–209; Fowl, *Philippians*, 9–10; Silva, *Philippians*, 5–7; Garland, "Philippians," 178–80; Blomberg, *Pentecost to Patmos*, 325–27. For information on prisons in the ancient Roman world and its significance for the letter to the Philippians, see Wansink, *Chained in Christ*; Bailey, "Perspectives from Prison," 83–97; Finlan, *Apostle Paul*, 136–37.

According to Acts, Paul and Timothy, together with Silas (and Luke?), spent some time in Philippi, described as a "first city of the region of Macedonia, a (Roman) colony" (Acts 16:12).[2] While in Philippi, Paul converted Lydia and her household (16:13–15), was briefly imprisoned together with Silas for exorcizing a slave girl (16:16–23), converted his Roman jailer along with his household (16:24–34), and was released when it was learned that both Paul and Silas were Roman citizens (16:35–40). The close relationship between Rome as the letter's provenance and Philippi as its destination comes into play within the letter's rhetorical dynamics in view of Philippi's special status as a Roman colony.[3]

Philippians as a Ritual of Worship

Introductory Worship

Paul and Timothy, as "slaves of Christ Jesus," send the letter "to all the holy ones in Christ Jesus who are in Philippi with the overseers and ministers" (Phil 1:1). The intended audience of the letter are thus all the "holy ones," that is, all those who are separated from the rest of Philippian society and consecrated to God, with the ability and responsibility of worshiping God. They are to worship God as "holy ones" who are "in Christ Jesus," that is, within the dynamic sphere or realm of existence established by the life, death, and resurrection of Christ Jesus. Among these "holy ones" addressed by the letter are their "overseers and ministers," those who have roles of leadership among them. They are those who supervise and assist the Philippian congregation to be the "holy ones" who offer both liturgical and ethical worship to God.[4]

The epistolary worship begins as Paul and Timothy pray that God, who has already graced the audience in making them holy ones in Christ Jesus (1:1b), will grant them yet further "grace" and peace (1:2) in, through, and after listening to the letter. This concept of the "grace"

2. On the difficulty of the translation here, see BDAG, 632.

3. Heil, *Philippians*. For more on Philippi at the time of the letter, see Bormann, *Philippi*; Pilhofer, *Philippi*; Oakes, *Philippians*, 1–54; Cassidy, *Four Times Peter*, 109–12; Hansen, *Philippians*, 1–6. On the social context of the Philippian Christian community, see Ascough, *Paul's Macedonian Associations*, 110–61.

4. Wagner, "Holiness and Community in Philippians," 257–74.

or "favor" (*charis*) of God is not only a gift from God but carries with it a connotation of divine empowerment or enablement.[5] God's grace has empowered the audience to become holy ones "in Christ Jesus" and will empower them to lives of liturgical and ethical worship as holy ones who are also "in Philippi."

Coupled with God's grace that Paul and Timothy pray to be given to their audience is "peace"—a state of overall well-being or harmony— that comes from God our Father and the Lord Jesus Christ (1:2). Paul and Timothy pray that with the grace of God their audience may live in peace with God, with one another as holy ones who are in Christ Jesus, and, as holy ones who are in Christ and in Philippi, with non-believers who are not in Christ Jesus but in Philippi, as well as with the overseers and ministers among them.[6] The progression that moves from Paul and Timothy as "slaves of Christ Jesus" (1:1a) to the Philippians as "holy ones in Christ Jesus" (1:1b) and climaxes with the prayer of grace and peace from "the Lord Jesus Christ" (1:2) serves as the dominant theme ringing in the ears of the audience, now poised for a renewed experience of this grace and peace as they listen to the rest of the letter.

Worship in the Thanksgiving Section

The opening address and greeting (1:1–2) is followed by a thanksgiving section beginning with the pronouncement that "I thank my God at every remembrance of you" (1:3). Paul's declaration that "I thank (*eucharistō*) my God" continues the epistolary worship, as Paul personally acknowledges and praises God for his "grace" (*charis*). The audience is assured that every time Paul remembers and thinks of them, with the implication that he thinks of them quite often, including while he is writing this letter, it is an occasion for Paul to offer an act of worship by rendering thanks and praise to God.[7]

5. "It is worth remembering that Paul links *charis* with the language of glory, wealth, mystery, and power" (Harrison, *Paul's Language of Grace*, 243).

6. "In Paul 'peace' can refer in turn to (1) peace with God (= cessation of hostilities), (2) peace within the believing community, (3) inner peace in place of turmoil, and (4) rest or order within a context of worship" (Fee, *Philippians*, 71n62).

7. "Thanking '*my* God' reflects Paul's personal relationship to God, whom he has identified as 'our Father' (1:2); it does not mean that he is thanking *his* God as opposed to other so-called gods" (Garland, "Philippians," 192).

Paul continues the introduction to the thanksgiving section of the letter with the words "always in my every petition on behalf of all of you" (1:4a). The audience are further assured not only that Paul thanks God at his frequent remembrances of them (1:3), but that each and every time that he does so it is in a special petition to God on behalf of "*all* of you" as a completely united community, "*all* the holy ones in Christ Jesus who are in Philippi" (1:1). Paul makes every special petition to God on behalf of his Philippian audience not only in a context of thanks and praise for the grace of God but with an emphasis on his joy in doing so: "making the petition with joy" (1:4b). This begins the theme of joy that dominates the letter and characterizes its worship, as the Greek word for "joy" (*chara*) is closely related to the word for "grace" and "thanks" (*charis*).[8]

The strong implication that the audience are at the basis of Paul's joyful praying to God for them is confirmed as he continues, "at your fellowship for the gospel from the first day until now" (1:5). The audience have now heard a primary reason for Paul's close relationship with them. He thanks God at every remembrance "of you" (1:3), and makes his petitions to God with a distinct joy on behalf of all "of you" (1:4), because of "your" mutual "fellowship" or "partnership" (*koinōnia*), both with Paul and with one another as a community united in and through their worship, for the gospel.

Paul then assures his audience of his confidence that his prayer on behalf of them will be answered: "having confidence of this very thing, that he who began in you a good work will perfect it until the day of Christ Jesus" (1:6). That God is the one who began this "good work" in the audience from the first "day" until the present time (1:5) assures them that God will also continue to perfect it all the way until the "day" of Christ Jesus, the "day" of his triumphant return in glory at the end of time. Paul's praying not only assures the audience of God's continual, complete, and final activity on their behalf, but also indirectly encour-

---

8. "Paul makes his petition 'with joy'; and the jubilant note struck here at the beginning rings throughout the whole letter (cf. 1:18, 25; 2:2, 17, 18 [twice], 28, 29; 3:1; 4:1, 4 [twice], 10)" (O'Brien, *Philippians*, 58). "The prepositional phrase describes the quality of Paul's prayer and is the first use of the root word *chara*, which characterizes the Philippian letter, Paul's epistle of joy and rejoicing. It is the only use of the word in Pauline thanksgivings and sets the emotional tone of this whole epistle" (Thurston, *Philippians*, 49).

ages them] to continue to play their own role in the "good work" of their fellowship with Paul and one another, which includes their communal worship, for the advancement of the gospel of Christ.

As a fellow sharer with the Philippians of "the grace" (1:7), Paul prays that they may properly respond to this divine grace with their ethical worship. To the God whom Paul invokes as his witness for how he longs for all of the Philippians with the affection of Christ Jesus (1:8), Paul prays that their love even more and more may abound in knowledge and every perception (1:9).[9] Then they may determine the things that really matter in the way that they conduct their lives, so that they may be morally "sincere" or "pure" as well as "faultless" for the day of Christ (1:10).[10] Paul's prayer then functions not only as a prayer for God to fulfill for the audience, but also as an indirect exhortation for the audience to play their part, with the help of God, to bring about the prayer's fulfillment.[11] Having been filled with "the fruit of the righteousness that is through Jesus Christ," that is, "the grace" they share with Paul, their being morally pure and faultless will constitute their response of ethical worship "for the glory and praise of God" (1:11). Paul wants his Philippian audience, through this thanksgiving section of the letter (1:3–11), to realize that what God has done, continues to do, and will do for them through and for Jesus Christ (1:6, 11a) is ultimately to lead them to worship—to the glory and praise of God himself (1:11b).[12]

---

9. "Paul frequently calls on God as *witness* to his thoughts, intentions, and prayers (Rom 1:9; Phil 1:8; 2 Cor 1:23; 1 Thess 2:5)" (Beutler, "*martys*," 394). "God is spoken of as a witness (*martys*) not in a judicial sense of witness to facts, but in a more general sense of his witnessing to the processes and motives in Paul's inner life" (O'Brien, *Philippians*, 71).

10. "[T]he prayer, after all, emphasizes 'love' not as 'affection' but as behavior, behavior that is both 'pure' (stemming from right motives) and 'blameless' (lacking offense)" (Fee, *Philippians*, 99).

11. "Paul's prayer is in effect a commandment that the Philippians give evidence of their sanctification now" (Silva, *Philippians*, 53).

12. "The apostle concludes his prayer report on a note of praise. His thanksgiving thus returns to the divine basis on which it had begun. God's saving work among the Philippians eventually redounds to the divine glory" (O'Brien, *Philippians*, 82).

Worship in the Body of the Letter

The Paul who prayed for the Philippians (1:4, 9) knows that the proclamation of Christ, in which he rejoices and will be joyful (1:18), will lead to his salvation through their prayer for him (1:19).[13] Paul then speaks of the outcome of his imprisonment in terms of his own ethical worship. He declares his hope that Christ will be "magnified," that is, "glorified" or "praised," in his body, whether through his life or through his death (1:20). Christ will be magnified and thus worshiped by Paul whether he is released from prison to continue preaching the gospel of Christ or put to death.[14]

Part of the Philippians' ethical worship is their selfless and humble way of thinking, their ethical mindset.[15] They are to fill up Paul's joy by thinking the same thing, having the same love, united in mind, thinking the one thing, nothing according to self-seeking nor according to vainglory, but in humility considering one another more important than themselves.[16] Each of them is to look out not for the things of themselves but for the things of others. They are thus to adopt the same way of humble thinking that is in Christ Jesus (2:2–5).[17] He offered pleasing ethical worship to God by not only becoming a human being

13. "He [Paul] does not believe he has the power to survive on his own without the prayer partnership of a supporting faith community. In listing the intercessory prayers of the Philippians as a contributing factor, he shows that he implicitly expects them to be unified in their prayers for him" (Garland, "Philippians," 202).

14. "Again, it is in line with the LXX use of the word when St. Paul speaks of magnifying Christ by his life or by his death, i.e., giving him glory and praise, because the Lord is exalted when the gospel is proclaimed" (Spicq, "*megaleîos*," 2.460)

15. On the verb "think," Fee (*Philippians*, 184–85) explains, "[T]he word does not mean 'to think' in the sense of 'cogitate'; rather it carries the nuance of 'setting one's mind on,' thus having a certain disposition toward something (e.g., life, values, people) or a certain way of looking at things, thus 'mindset.'"

16. "[I]t is not so much that others in the community are to be thought of as 'better than I am,' but as those whose needs and concerns 'surpass' my own" (ibid., 189).

17. "Grammatically, therefore, the simplest reading is to supply the *present* tense of 'to be': 'have this attitude amongst yourselves, which *is* also in Christ Jesus.' . . . this reading has the advantage that the indicated attitudes of the mind of Christ are seen to be not just a past fact of history but a *present reality*. . . . In some sense, therefore, the 'mind-set' of unselfish compassion which Paul encourages in the Philippians 'is present' in Christ Jesus both historically and eternally" (Bockmuehl, *Philippians*, 123–24). "The Philippians are either to imitate Christ or to be what they already are in him (or both!)" (Thurston, *Philippians*, 80). See also Burridge, *Imitating Jesus*, 146.

but by humbling himself, becoming obedient to God to the point of death on a cross (2:6–8). In response, God made him the focus of a universal worship: "therefore indeed God exalted him and granted him the name that is above every name, so that at the name of Jesus every knee should bend, of those in heaven and of those on earth and of those under the earth, and every tongue confess that Jesus Christ is Lord to the glory of God the Father" (2:9–11).[18]

The implication is that if the Philippians adopt a selfless, humble, Christ-like way of thinking as their habitual mindset, it will likewise lead to the worship that glorifies God. Indeed, God is the one working within them both to desire and to work for the sake of his good pleasure. They are to do everything without grumbling or questioning, so that they may become morally "blameless and innocent," children of God without moral "blemish" so that they may offer proper ethical worship to God as "holy ones" in the midst of a crooked and perverse generation, among whom they shine as lights in the world (2:13–15).

The Philippians then hear how Paul's joy in his labor, the joy that often accompanies and characterizes worship, is interrelated to their own: "But if indeed I am being poured out like a drink offering upon the sacrifice and service of your faith, I am rejoicing, indeed I am rejoicing with all of you. And in the same way you are to be rejoicing, indeed you are to be rejoicing with me" (2:17–18). Paul vividly describes the ordeal of his current imprisonment for the sake of defending and promoting the gospel as his "being poured out like a drink offering upon the sacrifice and service" of the audience's "faith" (2:17a).[19] This cultic metaphor expresses Paul's suffering through imprisonment for the gospel as his "being poured out" like a wine drink offering to the Lord upon the "sacrifice and service," that is, the "sacrificial service" of the audience's own suffering on behalf of Christ.[20] This and Paul's previ-

18. For a treatment of 2:6–11 that focuses especially on the significance of 2:9–11 for an indication of early worship of Jesus, see Hurtado, *How on Earth*, 83–107; idem, *Lord Jesus Christ*, 118–23.

19. "[I]t is best to consider *pisteōs* [faith] as the sacrificial service itself. The genitive is thus epexegetical, and the context demands that it be understood comprehensively . . . it embraces everything that made up their Christian life as a self-offering to God" (O'Brien, *Philippians*, 310).

20. "In both the Jewish cultus and pagan rites the libation was normally only an accompanying element to the sacrifice, and here too in Philippians 2:17 the weight of the verse falls not upon Paul's offering, but the sacrifice and service of the Philippians

ous assurance that he will remain with them for their advancement and joy in the "faith" (1:25) aim to motivate them not only to continue to demonstrate progress in the growth of their own faith but to work for the spread of the faith of the gospel of Christ to others. This is the "sacrificial" worship they may offer to God and in which they may rejoice together with Paul.[21]

The pointed assertion that not only is Paul "rejoicing with" all in his audience but that all of them are likewise to be "rejoicing with" him (2:17b–18) continues the theme of the joy that unites Paul and his audience in their mutual endeavor of advancing the gospel of Christ despite the suffering it may entail. This mutual endeavor constitutes their "sacrificial" worship that promotes their mutual joy.[22] The audience are to fill up Paul's "joy" by thinking the same thing, having the same love, being like-minded, thinking the one thing (2:2). Paul has assured his

---

over which Paul's offering is poured. . . . Paul thus portrays the Philippians as a community of priests" (Ware, *Philippians*, 272). "Paul links his 'being poured out' and the Philippians' sacrificial service, and he depicts them as priests at an altar, offering up the sacrificial gift of their faith. The image recalls their partnership in the defense and confirmation of the gospel (1:7) and suggests that both he and they are making sacrificial offerings (2:25, 30; 4:18)" (Garland, "Philippians," 227).

21. "In Paul's mind he has been put in prison according to God's will to defend the Gospel (Phil. 1.16). The result has been that the Gospel has advanced (1.12). . . . The Philippians on the other hand are suffering like Paul for 'holding out the word of life' (2.16). This is their ministry of faith (2.17). Paul by preaching in a difficult context (i.e. prison) is suffering but not complaining; rather rejoicing. Similarly Paul wants the Philippians to rejoice too (2.18) and not complain (2.14) or argue as they preach the Gospel. So Paul's wine-libation is his personally-costly (sic) preaching from prison which adds a pleasant aroma to the Philippians' sacrifice of ministering in a comparable difficult context. Together they share the same struggle as one person contending for the Gospel (1.27)" (Smith, *Timothy's Task*, 120–21).

22. "To this point every mention of 'joy,' except in 1:25, has had to do with Paul himself. With this imperative a subtle, but noteworthy, shift toward them takes place. What began in 1:25 as concern for their 'progress and *joy* regarding the faith' is now put into the form of an imperative, an imperative that will recur at further points in the rest of the letter; significantly, its first occurrence (1) is totally intertwined with Paul's joy, and (2) is found in the context of rejoicing in the midst of suffering and opposition. . . . Thus, the double repetition, even though it appears unnecessarily redundant, makes perfectly good sense both in the context of the whole letter and at this point in the 'argument.' What Paul is emphasizing in each case is that, first, he and they rejoice on their own accounts for the privilege of serving the gospel, even in the midst of great adversity, and second that they do so mutually, as they have done so much else mutually" (Fee, *Philippians*, 256).

audience that he, despite his present imprisonment, will remain beside all of them for their advancement and "joy" in the faith (1:25). And Paul has assured them that he makes every petition to God on behalf of them with "joy" at their fellowship with him for the gospel (1:4–5).

The letter's theme of a figurative "sacrificial" worship continues as Paul refers to Epaphroditus, whom he is sending back to the Philippians, as "your apostle and servant in my need" (2:25). Epaphroditus is not only their "apostle," the one sent by the Philippians with their gift of material support for the imprisoned Paul, but their "servant" (*leitourgon*), a word with a cultic connotation suggesting that he presented the gift from the Philippians as part of a figurative act of sacrificial worship. Epaphroditus was able to substitute for and represent the audience in filling up the lack of their cultic "service" (*leitourgias*) toward Paul due to their absence (2:30).[23] The filling up the audience's lack of cultic "service" toward Paul by Epaphroditus thus reinforces Paul's appeal for the audience to rejoice along with him because of his being poured out like a drink offering upon the sacrificial "service" (*leitourgia*) of their faith (2:17–18).

The suggestion that Epaphroditus is figuratively a cultic servant performing an act of sacrificial worship is confirmed as Paul acknowledges his reception of the gift from Epaphroditus sent to him by his Philippian audience: "For I have received in full everything and I am abounding. I have been filled up, having received from Epaphroditus the things from you, an aroma of fragrance, an acceptable sacrifice, pleasing to God" (4:18). This metaphorical characterization of the Philippians' gift as "an aroma of fragrance, an acceptable sacrifice (*thusian*), pleasing to God" (4:18), with its allusions to a recurrent formulaic phrase describing sacrifices to God in the Old Testament (cf. LXX Gen 8:21; Exod 29:18, 25, 41; Lev 1:9, 13, 17; Ezek 20:41), elaborates upon, as it resonates with, Paul's earlier reference to the "sacrifice" (*thusia*) and cultic service of the faith of his audience (2:17).[24] The gift the

23. "[W]hat is in focus is not the Philippians' shortcomings, but Epaphroditus' service. The point is that he is to be esteemed for risking his life in Christ's work and for his service to Paul. He, like Timothy, is an example of one who has lived the kind of life Paul commends to the Philippians in 2:1–4" (Thurston, *Philippians*, 105).

24. "The original imagery of *osmēn euōdias* ['aroma of fragrance'] is that of God taking pleasure in the odour from the sacrifices that his people offer him. The expression is then used figuratively of an offering (or those who offer it) that is pleas-

Philippians have sent to Paul through Epaphroditus exemplifies the "sacrifice" and cultic service of their faith. As a cultic service, this "sacrifice" is acceptable not only to Paul but constitutes an act of worship with which God is fully pleased.[25]

In striking contrast to his vilification of the Jewish practice of ritual circumcision as nothing more than a "mutilation" (3:2), Paul asserts that "we"—he, his audience, and all believers—are "the circumcision" (3:3a). The implication is that "we," who metaphorically are *the circumcision*, do not need to undergo the Jewish initiation rite of circumcision in order to offer proper worship to God. As "the circumcision," we are "the ones who by the Spirit of God are worshiping and boasting in Christ Jesus, and not having put confidence in the flesh" (3:3b). That in our relationship to and worship of God we believers, who "are the circumcision," depend not on the actual ritual of physical circumcision, which involves putting confidence "in the flesh," but on the "Spirit" of God (3:3), reminds the audience of the fellowship of "Spirit" they share with one another and with Paul (2:1) as fellow worshipers of God.

Worship in the Letter's Closing

As he begins to bring the letter to a close, Paul reassures his Philippian audience to "be anxious about nothing" (4:6a). Rather, "in everything, by prayer and petition, with thanksgiving," they are to let their requests be known before God (4:6). This directive regarding their thankful petitions in things concerning themselves develops Paul's previous confident hope regarding their petition for him, when he asserted, "for I know that this for me will lead to salvation through the petition of you and supply of the Spirit of Jesus Christ" (1:19). And it also further complements Paul's own thankful petitions for his Philippian audience, when he proclaimed, "I thank my God at every remembrance of you,

---

ing and acceptable to him" (O'Brien, *Philippians*, 541). "Paul has already referred to Epaphroditus's 'ministry' as a 'priestly service' [2:25–30] to Paul on their behalf. Here he spells out what that means with language borrowed directly from the LXX, used to indicate the interplay between the human and the divine in the sacrifices" (Fee, *Philippians*, 451).

25. "[O]ne is to recognize here not so much the general Greek background of 'service rendered' as the fulfillment of the true Christian 'worship' and the church's offering of 'sacrifices' pleasing to God" (Balz, "*leitourgia*," 349).

always in my every petition on behalf of all of you, making the petition with joy" (1:3–4). Paul's promise that "the peace of God that surpasses all understanding will guard your hearts and your minds in Christ Jesus" (4:7) reinforces, even as it elaborates upon, Paul's introductory prayer of "grace to you and peace from God our Father and the Lord Jesus Christ" (1:2). This promise regarding the peace of God is thus the direct result of the audience engaging in the communal worship of making known their requests before God (4:6), assuring them of its benefit, regardless of whether such requests are granted.[26]

Paul then adds a further directive regarding the kind of mental activity that accords with the promise about the peace of God (4:7): "Furthermore, brothers, whatever is true, whatever is honorable, whatever is right, whatever is pure, whatever is pleasing, whatever is commendable, if there is any excellence, and if there is any praise, these things consider" (4:8). This is the kind of thinking and mindset that is to be part of their ethical worship. The climactic conclusion of the list, "if there is any praise" recalls the "praise" of God through Jesus Christ in Paul's prayer that the audience may "determine the things that matter, so that you may be sincere and faultless for the day of Christ, having been filled up with the fruit of righteousness that is through Jesus Christ for the glory and praise of God" (1:10–11).

Paul's promise that "the God of peace will be with you" (4:9b) flows from and follows upon the things the audience are to consider and the things they are to practice in imitation of Paul (4:8–9a) as part of their ethical worship. This reinforces and complements Paul's previous assurance to the audience of the benefit of their liturgical worship. Paul's previous promise to the audience, as a response to their liturgical worship of making their requests known to God by prayer and petition, with thanksgiving (4:6), was that the peace of God that surpasses all understanding will then guard their hearts and their minds in Christ

26. "[A]s a consequence of the Philippians letting their requests be made known to God with thanksgiving, his peace will guard them. V. 7 is not a concluding wish . . . it is a specific and certain promise about God's peace that is attached to the encouraging admonition of v. 6. Most significantly, this promise about God's peace guarding the Philippians is given irrespective of whether their concrete requests are granted or not. This word of assurance is independent of their petitions being answered by God in the affirmative. God's peace will be powerfully at work in their lives as a result (*kai*) of their pouring out their hearts in petition with thanksgiving, not because they have made requests that are perfectly in line with the will of God" (O'Brien, *Philippians*, 495–96).

Jesus (4:7). That promise is now climactically intensified in its personal dimensions. Not only will "the peace of God," the profound peace that comes from God, guard "your" hearts and "your" minds—the center and core of their beings, but "the God of peace," the very person of the God who is the source of that profound peace, will be "with you"— present with the very persons themselves of those in the audience at Philippi.[27]

In reciprocation for their act of worship, the sacrificial gift of his Philippian audience, which is well pleasing "to God " (4:18b), the "God" before whom the audience are to make known their requests (4:6), Paul promises that "my God will fill up your every need" (4:19a). Paul's promise here thus bolsters and develops his previous promises that "the peace of God that surpasses all understanding will guard your hearts and your minds" (4:7) and "the God of peace will be with you" (4:9). That God "will fill up" your every "need" reciprocates not only for the filling up of Paul—"I have been filled up"—by their sacrificial gift now while he is in prison (4:18a), but for their having sent "to me in my need" when Paul was in Thessalonica (4:16). That God will fill up "your" every need reciprocates for "the things from you" that Paul has received from Epaphroditus (4:17).

In his climactic closing doxology, "To our God and Father, glory to the ages of the ages, Amen!" (4:20), Paul leads his Philippian congregation in the communal worship of rendering praise to God as reciprocation for his promise that "God will fill up your every need" (4:19). And it complements his acknowledgment of his audience's sacrificial gift to him as "well pleasing to God" (4:18). The employment of the first-person plural pronoun in the address of the doxology, "to *our* God and Father," further unites the audience with Paul and all other believers, as it flows progressively from the use of the first-person singular and second-person plural pronouns in Paul's promise that "*my* God will fill up *your* every need" (4:19), recalling Paul's previous pronouncement that "I thank *my* God at every remembrance of *you*" (1:3). The audi-

---

27. "At v. 7 they were promised that God's peace would keep them safe; here they are assured that the God of peace himself will be with them. The two promises are similar, with only a slight difference of emphasis: in the former, the focus is upon God's salvation guarding them; in the latter, it is upon his presence to bless and to save them. Since the gift of his peace cannot be separated from his presence as the giver, these two assurances are closely related in meaning" (ibid., 512).

ence are to appreciate that the God whom Paul serves as "*my* God" is also "*our* God," the God and Father of Paul, the audience, and all other believers, the God to whom glory is due forever.[28]

The transition from Paul's promise for the audience, with its reference to "in *glory* in Christ Jesus" (4:19b), to his doxology, "to our God and Father, *glory* to the ages of the ages, Amen!" (4:20), further leads his audience into the praise of God, based on what God has accomplished for them and all believers in Christ Jesus. At the beginning of the letter the audience heard Paul's prayer for them, namely, "that your love even more and more may abound in knowledge and every perception in order that you determine the things that matter, so that you may be sincere and faultless for the day of Christ, having been filled up with the fruit of righteousness that is through Jesus Christ for the *glory* and praise of God" (1:9–11). Later they heard him proclaim the climactic hymnic conclusion "that at the name of Jesus every knee should bend, of those in heaven and of those on earth and of those under the earth, and every tongue confess that Jesus Christ is Lord to the *glory* of God the Father" (2:10–11). And now, the audience are invited to join Paul in his praise that to *our* God, the God who will fill up the audience's "every need according to his wealth in *glory* in Christ Jesus" (4:19), is "*glory* to the ages of the ages, Amen!" (4:20).[29]

Paul concludes the letter with his own final greeting for the audience: "The grace of the Lord Jesus Christ with your spirit!" (4:23). This verbless greeting affirms the grace the Philippian audience have already received before hearing the letter as well as the renewed experience of that grace which the hearing of the letter has just provided them. It also functions as a prayer that they continue to experience this grace after and as a result of hearing the letter.

At the beginning of the letter Paul greeted the audience with the prayerful wish of "grace to you and peace from God our Father and

---

28. As O'Brien (ibid., 545n213) points out, "my God" means "'the God whom I serve', not 'the God whom I possess.'"

29. "To give God glory is not to add something that is not already present; it is rather an active acknowledgment or extolling of what he is or has already done" (ibid., 550). "Paul's final Amen confirms that this doxology is no mere rhetorical flourish, but gives voice to his own deep conviction. It is the appropriately worshipful response to God's generous and sovereign providence in Christ Jesus" (Bockmuehl, *Philippians,* 267).

the Lord Jesus Christ" (1:2). The audience were then made aware of how they are already fellow sharers with Paul of "the grace" (1:7). Now, after the stirring doxology to "our God and Father" (4:20), the focus is more directly on the "grace" as coming from "the Lord Jesus Christ" (4:23). The audience are to appreciate that Paul's prayer is for the grace that comes from "the Lord Jesus Christ," as the Lord whom all believers await as their savior (3:20). They are to appreciate that Paul's prayer is for the "grace" that comes from "Christ Jesus my Lord," the surpassing greatness of the knowledge of whom has prompted Paul to consider everything else as worthless (3:8). And they are to appreciate that Paul's prayer is for the "grace" that comes from the "Jesus Christ" whom God "granted" or "graced" with the name above every name (2:9), so that every tongue is to confess him as "Lord" to the glory of God the Father (2:11).[30]

Paul's prayer is that the grace of the Lord Jesus Christ be "with your spirit" (4:23), that is, with the human "spirit" that animates and is synonymous with their persons and that embraces their way of thinking, which has been such a central focus in the letter. The grace of the Lord Jesus Christ is to be with the human spirit of the audience, who are part of the fellowship of the divine "Spirit" (2:1). It is by this divine "Spirit of God" that they worship and boast in Christ Jesus (3:3). They are to be standing firm in this "one Spirit" (1:27). Indeed, Paul is confident of salvation through the supply of the "Spirit of Jesus Christ" himself (1:19). The "grace" that comes from Jesus Christ thus includes the "Spirit" that comes from Jesus Christ. Hence, Paul's prayer that the grace of the Lord Jesus Christ be with the "spirit" of each individual member of the audience is the prayer for the grace that will enable each of them to adopt the same selfless and humble mindset (2:2–5) that resulted in God's exaltation of Jesus Christ as the Lord at the focus of a universal worship (2:6–11).[31]

---

30. "The phrase ['the grace of the Lord Jesus Christ'] describes not a character or quality of Jesus but something he shows and does. The Lord Jesus who is the source of grace bestows it freely on the congregation at Philippi. It will sustain the community, for it is by grace alone that they will stand" (O'Brien, *Philippians*, 555).

31. "[T]he distributive singular, 'with your (pl.) spirit (sing.),' in effect, as with the first of the greetings in v. 21, individualizes the grace-benediction, so that each of them (in the 'spirit' of each) will experience the desired grace that is here prayed for" (Fee, *Philippians*, 461).

Conclusion: Worship in Philippians

The epistolary worship of the letter to the Philippians begins as Paul and Timothy pray that God, who has already graced the audience in making them holy ones in Christ Jesus (1:1b), will grant them yet further "grace" and peace (1:2) in, through, and after listening to the letter. Through the thanksgiving section (1:3–11) of this letter that will be characterized by the joy that accompanies worship (1:4) Paul wants his Philippian audience to realize that what God has done, continues to do, and will do for them through and for Jesus Christ (1:6, 11a) is ultimately to lead them to joyous worship—to the glory and praise of God himself (1:11b).

In the body of the letter Paul assures his audience that Christ will be magnified and thus worshiped by Paul whether he is released from prison to continue preaching the gospel of Christ or put to death (1:20). As a model for the audience, Christ offered pleasing ethical worship to God by not only becoming a human being but by humbling himself, becoming obedient to God to the point of death on a cross (2:6–8). In response, God made him the focus of a universal worship: "therefore indeed God exalted him and granted him the name that is above every name, so that at the name of Jesus every knee should bend, of those in heaven and of those on earth and of those under the earth, and every tongue confess that Jesus Christ is Lord to the glory of God the Father" (2:9–11). If the Philippians' adopt a selfless, humble, Christ-like way of thinking as their habitual mindset, it will likewise lead to the worship that glorifies God.

Paul vividly describes the ordeal of his current imprisonment for the sake of defending and promoting the gospel as his "being poured out like a drink offering upon the sacrifice and service" of the audience's "faith" (2:17a). This cultic metaphor expresses Paul's suffering through imprisonment for the gospel as his "being poured out" like a wine drink offering to the Lord upon the "sacrifice and service," that is, the "sacrificial service" of the audience's own suffering on behalf of Christ. This is the "sacrificial" worship they may offer to God and in which they may rejoice together with Paul. The filling up the audience's lack of cultic "service" toward Paul (2:30) by Epaphroditus, their cultic "servant" (2:25), reinforces Paul's appeal for the audience to rejoice along with him because of his being poured out like a drink offering upon the sacrificial "service" of their faith (2:17–18).

The metaphorical characterization of the Philippians' gift to Paul as "an aroma of fragrance, an acceptable sacrifice, pleasing to God" (4:18), elaborates upon, as it resonates with, Paul's earlier reference to the "sacrifice" and cultic service of the faith of his audience (2:17). The gift the Philippians have sent to Paul through Epaphroditus exemplifies the "sacrifice" and cultic service of their faith. As a cultic service, this "sacrifice" is acceptable not only to Paul but constitutes an act of worship with which God is fully pleased.

As "the circumcision," we believers are "the ones who by the Spirit of God are worshiping and boasting in Christ Jesus, and not having put confidence in the flesh" (3:3). That in our relationship to and worship of God we believers depend not on the actual ritual of physical circumcision, which involves putting confidence "in the flesh," but on the "Spirit" of God, reminds the audience of the fellowship of "Spirit" they share with one another and with Paul (2:1) as fellow worshipers of God.

As the letter comes to a close, Paul's promise that "the peace of God that surpasses all understanding will guard your hearts and your minds in Christ Jesus" (4:7) reinforces, even as it elaborates upon, Paul's introductory prayer of "grace to you and peace from God our Father and the Lord Jesus Christ" (1:2). This promise regarding the peace of God is thus the direct result of the audience engaging in the communal worship of making known their requests before God (4:6), assuring them of its benefit, regardless of whether such requests are granted. Paul's promise, which flows from and follows upon the things the audience are to consider and the things they are to practice in imitation of Paul (4:8–9a) as part of their ethical worship, is that "the God of peace will be with you" (4:9b). Not only will "the peace of God," the profound peace that comes from God, guard "your" hearts and "your" minds—the center and core of their beings—but "the God of peace," the very person of the God who is the source of that profound peace, will be "with you"—present with the very persons themselves of those in the audience at Philippi.

In his climactic closing doxology, "To our God and Father, glory to the ages of the ages, Amen!" (4:20), Paul leads his Philippian congregation in the communal worship of rendering praise to God as reciprocation for his promise that "God will fill up your every need" (4:19). And it complements his acknowledgment of his audience's sacrificial gift to him as "well pleasing to God" (4:18). Paul's final greeting, a prayer that the "grace" of the Lord Jesus Christ be with the "spirit" of each individual member of the audience (4:23), resonates with the letter's initial prayer-greeting for divine "grace" (1:2) to frame the entire letter within a context of prayerful worship. It is a prayer for the grace that will enable each one of them to adopt the same selfless and humble mindset (2:2–5) that resulted in God's exaltation of Jesus Christ as the Lord at the focus of a universal worship of God (2:6–11).

Titus

Because they contain certain thematic and stylistic similarities, the three Pauline letters of Titus, 1 and 2 Timothy are often grouped together under the name of "the Pastoral Epistles." A more precise designation for them would be "Paul's letters to coworkers" or "Paul's letters to delegates." But they are not purely personal letters. The letter to Titus is indirectly addressed to the churches on Crete by directly addressing Titus. Similarly, the letters to Timothy are indirectly addressed to the churches in Ephesus by directly addressing Timothy. Each of these letters concludes with a greeting to a plural "you," confirming that they have been addressed to the whole community by addressing the individuals Titus and Timothy, respectively.

Many scholars in modern times have considered these letters, despite their self-presentation as authored and sent by Paul, to be pseudepigraphical with a pseudonymous author, and thus not authentically Pauline.[1] Their Pauline authorship, however, was never questioned in the early church. While there are certainly examples of pseudepigraphical works at the time of Paul, they are usually not actual letters used in correspondence. And their pseudonymous authors are revered figures of the ancient past (e.g., Enoch, Abraham, etc.), not someone who has died in the relatively recent past. If these letters are pseudonymous, they would have been intended to deceive their original audiences regarding their authenticity, and evidently succeeded in doing so until modern times. But, since literary property was important in the ancient world, and apostolic authorship and authority was highly valued among first-century Christians, it is unlikely that these letters are pseudonymous.

---

1. Wilder, "Pseudonymity," 28–51.

In short, theories of pseudonymity create more problems regarding the reconstruction of the historical context of these letters than do theories of their authenticity. The stylistic and linguistic differences between these three letters and the other Pauline letters can plausibly be explained as due to the different nature and time of the correspondence, that is, letters to churches through delegates of Paul, and/or a different amanuensis. Luke, a close companion of Paul, especially in his later years (2 Tim 4:11), is a possible candidate as the one who actually composed these letters as dictated and/or authorized by Paul.[2] It is also possible that Paul altered his style at this later stage of his life and ministry. At any rate, the view taken here is that these three letters addressed to delegates are authentically authored by Paul.[3]

The period after Paul's release from his imprisonment in Rome, the imprisonment narrated at the conclusion of the Acts of the Apostles, during which, in all probability, he authored the letter sent to the Philippians, provides a plausible historical context for his further apostolic ministry on Crete and in Ephesus, which preceded the letters to Titus and Timothy. Titus, a Greek believer not required to become Jewish by being circumcised, accompanied and worked with Paul (Gal 2:1–3), acting as Paul's envoy in his troubled relationship with the Corinthians. He visited Corinth several times and eventually delivered 2 Corinthians. He was part of the delegation charged with completing the collection for the mother church of Jerusalem (2 Cor 8:16–24). Paul describes Titus's conduct toward the Corinthians in this difficult period as exemplary (2 Cor 12:18). Despite his key relationship with Paul, Titus is never mentioned in the Acts of the Apostles.[4]

In the letter Paul addressed to him, Titus is to serve as Paul's delegate on the island of Crete (Titus 1:5). With sound doctrine Titus is to exhort believers and refute opponents. To help him in this task he is to appoint qualified leaders throughout the cities of Crete.[5] The let-

2. Riesner, "Pastoral Epistles," 239–58.

3. For recent discussions favorable toward the Pauline authenticity of the letters of Titus, 1 and 2 Timothy, see Fee, *1 and 2 Timothy, Titus*, 23–26; Knight, *Pastoral Epistles*, 21–52; Mounce, *Pastoral Epistles*, cxviii–cxxix; Johnson, *Letters to Timothy*, 55–99; Witherington, *Letters*, 23–38, 49–68; Towner, *Timothy and Titus*, 9–89. See also Donfried, "Rethinking Scholarly Approaches to 1 Timothy," 153–82; Köstenberger, "Pastoral Epistles," 1–27.

4. Walton, "Titus," 609.

5. Wieland, "Roman Crete," 338–54.

ter addresses not only Titus but the community of believers gathered to listen to the letter within a context of liturgical worship. They hear Paul authorizing and instructing Titus for the duties he is to perform as Paul's delegate, and for which they are to hold Titus accountable. But they also hear how they are to respond to the authority given to Titus and cooperate in the performance of his duties.

Titus as a Ritual of Worship

Introductory Worship

At the outset Paul establishes the letter's context of communal worship when he introduces himself as the slave of God and apostle of Jesus Christ entrusted with the word that proclaims the hope of eternal life according to the command of "our" savior, God. After then addressing Titus as "a genuine child according to a common faith," Paul pronounces, not just to Titus but to the whole community, the initial greeting of grace and peace from God the Father and Christ Jesus, "our" savior (1:1–4). In other words, both God and Jesus Christ are "*our*" savior—the savior not only of Paul and Titus but of all, especially of those gathered as a worshiping assembly to listen to this letter.[6] This initial greeting not only affirms the divine grace and peace that Titus and the Cretans received when they became believers but prays that they will have a renewed and deepened experience of this divine grace as they listen to the letter.

Worship in the Body of the Letter

One of the key ways of performing ethical worship according to this letter is the doing of "commendable works" (*kalōn ergōn*), that is, good or noble deeds that are able to be praised by both human beings and God, and thus serve to render praise to God as acts of ethical worship.[7] Titus

6. Couser, "Sovereign Savior," 105–36; Wieland, *Significance of Salvation*, 183–238; idem, "Function of Salvation," 153–72.

7. For the connotations of "good, noble, praiseworthy, contributing to salvation" in the phrase "commendable works," see BDAG, 504. According to Towner (*Timothy and Titus*, 212), what the emphasis on observable Christian living in this phrase seeks to do is "to position authentic Christian existence within the world as that manner of life

himself is not only to be a model of "commendable works" (2:7), but to appoint as overseers of the churches, the worshiping communities, on Crete similar models of commendable works—men "able both to exhort with sound doctrine and reprove those who contradict" (1:9).[8] The worshiping assembly hear the "commendable works" they are to perform as their ethical worship in response to God's grace of saving all human beings, when Paul tells Titus, "Remind them to be subject to ruling authorities, to be obedient, to be ready for every good work, to revile no one, to be uncontentious, kind, demonstrating complete gentleness toward all human beings" (3:1–2).

The reception of divine grace from God the Father and Jesus Christ our savior that Paul affirmed for his audience and prayed that they continue to receive (1:4) serves as their inspiration and motivation for their life of worship. Paul declares: "The grace of God has appeared, saving all human beings, training us, so that, rejecting ungodliness and worldly desires, we might live sensibly and justly and godly in the present age, awaiting the blessed hope, the appearance of the glory of the great God and our savior, Jesus Christ, who gave himself on behalf of us, so that he might redeem us from all lawlessness and cleanse for himself a special people, zealous for commendable works" (2:11–14). This saving grace of God that is with them is the grace to which they are to respond as an assembly that worships not only liturgically but ethically. This grace that saves all human beings motivates the Cretan audience for the ethical worship of living "sensibly and justly and godly" and of performing works "commendable" to all human beings and the God who has saved them. Such commendable works serve as the ethical worship that not only praises God but attracts others to the praise of God.[9]

Paul continues to impress upon Titus how he is to insist upon the things regarding the grace that comes from our savior, God, and through Jesus Christ, our savior. This divine saving grace is to issue

---

determined by faith in Christ that is in accordance with the values and aims of God." See also Madsen, "Pastoral Epistles," 219–40.

8. Merkle, "Pastoral Epistles," 173–98.

9. According to Towner (*Timothy and Titus*, 765–66), "that very life of godliness, lived in the present age until hope has been fulfilled, has proved to be the goal of the Messiah's redemptive self-offering. The life of virtue that the Greeks idealized and the Cretan teachers diluted Paul here declares to be the realistic potential of those who respond to the one true God in faith." See also Ho, "Pastoral Epistles," 241–67.

in a response by believers of commendable works that serve as ethical worship: "But when the kindness and the love for human beings of our savior, God, appeared, not from works that we had done in righteousness, rather, according to his mercy, he saved us through a bath of rebirth and renewal of the Holy Spirit, whom he poured out on us richly through Jesus Christ, our savior, so that, justified by that grace, we might become heirs according to the hope of eternal life. Faithful is the word. And about these things I want you to insist, so that they who have believed in God may be intent to engage in commendable works" (3:4–8a).[10]

Worship in the Letter's Closing

After a final exhortation for the Cretan believers to learn to engage fruitfully in the "commendable works" that serve as ethical worship in praise of God (3:14), Paul closes the letter with a final prayer-greeting: "The grace with all of you!" (3:15). Although the letter has been directly addressed to Titus (1:4), it now becomes emphatically and climactically clear that it has been indirectly addressed to and heard by all of the Cretan believers who are gathered together in the liturgical assembly.

The greeting of "the grace with all of you" not only reaffirms that the Cretans have already received and accepted with faith the divine saving grace, but prays that, after and as a result of having listened to the letter, they may continue to experience this great saving grace. The "grace" that has been, is, and will be with all of the Cretan believers recalls the saving and merciful grace that comes from our savior God and through our savior Jesus Christ (3:4–6), the "grace" by which we believers are justified (3:7), so that we may be intent to engage in the commendable works (3:8a) by which we perform the ethical worship that gives praise to God. It recalls the "grace" of God that has appeared,

---

10. "This provides yet another illustration of the dominant theme in Titus, that right theology and right practice are inextricably bound together. . . . an understanding of the full plan of salvation leads believers necessarily into a daily living out of their commitment to the Lord. To separate the two is nonsensical" (Mounce, *Pastoral Epistles*, 452). "Thus the teaching process (3:1–2, 8) is intended to bring believers to a holistic expression of their faith in God, an expression that incorporates the cognitive (faith) and practical (action) dimensions into a visibly distinct manner of life" (Towner, *Timothy and Titus*, 792).

saving all human beings (2:11), and is training us so that, rejecting ungodliness and worldly desires, we might live sensibly and justly and godly in the present age (2:12). And it recalls the "grace" that brings with it "peace," the divine gift of overall well-being, that comes from God the Father and Christ Jesus, our savior (1:4). These prayer-greetings of "grace" at the beginning (1:4) and end (3:15) of the letter thus enclose the entire letter within a context of prayerful worship.[11]

Conclusion: Worship in Titus

The letter's initial greeting not only affirms the divine grace and peace that Titus and the Cretans received when they became believers but prays that they will have a renewed and deepened experience of this divine grace as they listen to the letter in their liturgical assembly (1:4). This saving grace of God that is with them is the grace to which they are to respond as an assembly that worship not only liturgically but ethically. This grace that saves all human beings motivates the Cretan audience for the ethical worship of living "sensibly and justly and godly" (2:12) and of performing works "commendable" to all human beings and the God who has saved them (2:14). Such commendable works serve as the ethical worship that not only praises God but attracts others to the praise of God. The "grace" that has been, is, and will be with all of the Cretan believers (3:15) recalls the saving and merciful grace that comes from our savior God and through our savior Jesus Christ (3:4–6), the "grace" by which we believers are justified (3:7), so that we may be intent to engage in the commendable works (3:8a) that epitomize authentic Christian living and by which we perform the ethical worship that gives praise to God. The prayer-greetings of "grace" at the beginning (1:4) and end (3:15) of the letter enclose the entire letter within a context of prayerful worship.

11. "The grace-wish is not a literary formality, but rather a genuine prayer or blessing that desires for the recipients the full experience of God's gracious and loving presence (with all this entails). 'All' extends the blessing to the churches under Titus's charge. Given the kinds of moral, social, and ecclesiastical challenges facing the young Cretan churches, and given the goal of actualizing faith in dynamic Christian living that Paul has set before them, this wish for a holistic experience of God's grace was nothing less than a final prayer for strength in battle" (Towner, *Timothy and Titus*, 805).

1 Timothy

Timothy, a Christian disciple who was an uncircumcised Jew, with a Jewish mother and Greek father, before being circumcised and joining Paul (Acts 16:1–3; cf. 2 Tim 1:5), was not only a co-sender with Paul of six letters (2 Corinthians, Philippians, Colossians, 1 and 2 Thessalonians, and Philemon) but also the recipient of two letters from Paul (1 and 2 Timothy). In the first letter Paul addressed to him, possibly from Macedonia, Timothy is to serve as Paul's delegate in Ephesus. Authorized with the instructions Paul will give him in the letter, Timothy is to command certain persons not to teach divisively (1 Tim 1:3).[1] Addressing the letter indirectly to the churches in Ephesus by addressing it directly to Timothy bestows upon Timothy the authority he needs to carry out Paul's instructions, as well as provides the epistolary Ephesian audience the criteria by which to hold him responsible for doing this.

1 Timothy as a Ritual of Worship

Introductory Worship

Paul introduces himself as "an apostle of Christ Jesus according to the command of God our savior and Christ Jesus our hope" (1:1). He thus begins this epistolary ritual of worship by drawing his audience into a

---

1. "[E]verything in the letter has to do with 1:3 ('As I urged you when I went to Macedonia, stay there in Ephesus so that you may command certain [people] not to teach false doctrines any longer') . . . this expresses both the occasion and the purpose of 1 Timothy. . . . this not only makes sense of every detail in the letter, but also helps to explain the nature and content of Titus and 2 Timothy as well" (Fee, *1 and 2 Timothy, Titus*, 7).

communal confession of faith in God as "our" savior and in Christ Jesus as "our" hope. After addressing Timothy as "a genuine child in faith," Paul pronounces the initial ritualistic greeting, praying that through the letter not only Timothy but the entire Christian community in Ephesus (1:3) may be the recipients of grace, mercy, and peace from God the Father and Christ Jesus "our" Lord (1:2)—the Lord of all believers.[2]

Distinctive to this prayer-greeting is the inclusion of "mercy" (*eleos*) to provide a specific focus for the grace. This divine "mercy" motivates Paul's own worship, which serves as a paradigm for all believers of thanksgiving and praise for God's gracious mercy. He declares the "gratitude," literally the "grace" (*charin*), he has for Christ Jesus "our" Lord because he considered Paul faithful in appointing him to ministry (1:12). Although formerly being a blasphemer, a persecutor, and an arrogant man, Paul was treated with "mercy" (*ēleēthēn*) because, being ignorant, he acted in unbelief (1:13). After acknowledging that the "grace" of "our" Lord superabounded, along with the faith and love that are in Christ Jesus (1:14), Paul confesses that "Christ Jesus came into the world to save sinners, of whom I am the first, I myself (1:15). But because of this I was treated with mercy (*ēleēthēn*), so that in me as the first Christ Jesus might demonstrate all patience as a prototype for those coming to believe in him for eternal life" (1:16). Paul brings his confession to a climax as he leads his audience in a stirring act of doxological worship: "To the king of the ages, immortal, invisible, the only God, honor and glory to the ages of the ages. Amen!" (1:17). The final "Amen" invites the audience to join in and affirm this act of worship by adding their own reverberating "Amen!"[3]

---

2. "By means of the plural pronoun 'our' (*hēmōn*), Paul joins his readers and himself in their union with each other as Christians, which is entailed in their mutual relationship to God as Savior and Father and Christ Jesus as Savior and Hope" (Knight, *Pastoral Epistles*, 62).

3. "It is fitting and usual for Paul, having reflected upon God's grace and mercy and what he has done for him, to burst into a doxology of praise. While this doxology stresses the transcendent nature of God, this only serves to heighten Paul's amazement that God would, in his mercy and grace, stoop to save a sinner such as Paul" (Mounce, *Pastoral Epistles*, 59). "The concluding 'amen' gives Timothy and the church the invitation to join in the acknowledgment" (Towner, *Timothy and Titus*, 154).

Instructions for Worship

This first letter to Timothy abounds with instructions for worship. Paul exhorts "that petitions, prayers, intercessions, and thanksgivings be made on behalf of all human beings, on behalf of kings and all those who are in authority, that we may lead a quiet and tranquil life in all godliness and dignity" (2:1–2). The noteworthy reference to all "godliness" (*eusebeia*) here denotes public behavior that embraces both liturgical and ethical worship.[4] Paul concludes that "this is commendable and acceptable before our savior, God, who wants all human beings to be saved and to come to a knowledge of truth" (2:3–4). That such behavior is "acceptable" (*apodekton*), a cultic term to describe proper sacrifices, underlines its character as ethical worship.[5]

Paul goes on to provide instructions for how the men are to conduct themselves for worship. He "wants,"—a word that has the authoritative force of an apostolic command—that they pray "in every place" (2:8a), in appropriate correspondence to his emphasis on universal salvation (2:1–7). In their praying they are to lift up "holy" or "pure" (*hosious*) hands without anger and dispute (2:8b). Their hands are thus to be "purified" for proper liturgical worship by making sure that their

---

4. According to Mounce (*Pastoral Epistles*, 83), Spicq (*Saint Paul*, 1.362) defines *eusebeia* as being "totally consecrated to God, to his worship, and to the fulfillment of his will . . . and it places emphasis on the outward appearances of worship and piety in honor of God . . . [and denotes] an extreme devotion to accomplish the divine will." According to Towner (*Timothy and Titus*, 173), "it dominates the emotions to lead one to worship and other aspects of appropriate conduct." "In conclusion, we should stress that in Greco-Roman, Jewish and Christian discussion, the term *eusebeia* and its cognates are used to refer to both belief and behavior, both reverence and action, including ritual action. It is not an either-or matter" (Witherington, *Letters*, 102). "[I]n general usage *eusebeia* came to mean the actual worship paid to the gods in cultic activities rather than a reverent attitude, although outward actions were seen as the expression of inner attitudes" (Trebilco, *Ephesus*, 361). See also Standhartinger, "*Eusebeia*," 51–82.

5. According to Towner (*Timothy and Titus*, 176), the word "acceptable" here "calls to mind the use of the word group in Leviticus to describe sacrifices as 'acceptable' to God. The effect of placing the activity of prayer into this OT legal and cultic framework is to underline its intrinsic importance to God and to his people by comparing it with the role of sacrifices in the old system. Prayer has replaced sacrifice for the messianic people of God." On the theme of salvation in 1 Timothy, see Wieland, *Significance of Salvation*, 19–106.

ethical conduct is free of anger and disputes, in contrast to the divisiveness of the false teachers (1:3).[6]

The instructions for the men, who are husbands, are complemented by instructions for the women, who are wives (cf. 2:13–15).[7] When they come to the liturgical gathering for worship, they are "to adorn themselves in respectable attire with modesty and prudence, not in braided hair and gold or pearls or expensive clothing, but as is proper for women who profess reverence to God through good works" (2:9–10).[8] Thus, the virtues of modesty and prudence in their attire are appropriate for their proper liturgical worship. Also, they are to be engaged in the doing of good works for their proper ethical worship, in accord with their professed claim of "reverence to God" (*theosebeian*).[9]

Those who aspire to roles of leadership in the church, to the services of "overseeing" and "ministering," which would include supervis-

---

6. "*Hosios* is thus taken over as an original expression of cultic purity and is applied to one's entire way of life and disposition" (Balz, "*hosios*," 536). "Paul is specifically concerned about the holiness and demeanor of men when they pray. This is set out in positive terms first by reference to the symbolic gesture of raising the hands in prayer (coupled with allusion to the rite of hand washing to signify purity). The background is the biblical tradition in which prayers in various contexts (invoking God's intervention, pronouncing blessing on others) were accentuated by the raising or extending of hands. . . . The visible public act of purification signified the presumed inward condition of purity/holiness of those about to engage in ministry. From the act and its significance, the image of 'purified hands' acquired metaphorical status in its reference to moral purity . . . The combination of the adjective 'holy/pure' and the symbolic gesture depicts one who is completely (outwardly and inwardly) ready for ministry" (Towner, *Timothy and Titus*, 201–2).

7. Köstenberger, "Interpretation of 1 Timothy 2:15," 107–44; Cohick, *Women*, 138–40.

8. Batten, "Neither Gold Nor Braided Hair," 484–501.

9. "This section has discussed the significance of two dress codes (2:9–11). The first was apparel characterised by gold and pearls and extravagant clothing that signalled to others a sexually lax lifestyle. The second did not describe an actual dress code but rather used the concept of adornment as a metaphor for the virtues of a wife who was not only godly but also adorned her life with good works" (Winter, *Roman Wives*, 108). "The content of the claim is expressed with the term *theosebeia*. It is equivalent to the term *eusebeia*, which defines authentic Christian existence as the integration of faith in God and the behavior that demonstrates this. Its selection here over the more frequently used term may correspond to the specific reference to wives (or to the language of the claim they were making), but in any case it indicates a claim to be authentic worshipers of God" (Towner, *Timothy and Titus*, 210). See also Mitchell, "Corrective Composition," 41–62.

ing and facilitating the communal worship, must practice appropriate social virtues. They should exhibit such commendable ethical behavior as being irreproachable, faithful spouses, temperate, prudent, respectable, hospitable, able to teach, not drunken, not aggressive, but gentle, uncontentious, not loving money (3:2–3, 8–12). They should be able to manage their own households well (3:3), "for if someone does not know how to manage his own household, how will he care for the church of God?" (3:5). They should also have a good reputation with those outside of the community (3:7). Indeed, those who minister commendably in the community, including the services they perform for the worship of the assembly, obtain much publicity that attracts people to faith in Christ Jesus, and thus play their role in advancing the cause of universal salvation (3:13).

Confessing the Great Mystery of Godliness

These things, including the instructions for worship, Paul is writing to Timothy, hoping to come to him and the Ephesian community in haste (3:14). But if he should be delayed, they are to know how it is necessary to behave in the household of God, which is the church of the living God, the pillar and foundation of the truth (3:15).[10] Such behavior includes the proper worship of the one and only "living God."[11] Although absent, Paul, through the letter as a substitute for his personal presence, leads Timothy and the community in such worship of the "living God." Since "confessedly" (*homologoumenōs*), that is, "undeniably" and able to be confessed by everyone, great is the mystery of godliness (3:16a), Paul leads his audience in an epistolary confession of this "great" (*mega*)

10. "Now it seems likely that Paul's purpose for writing Timothy is broader than just dealing with the false teachers in an ad hoc situation—he is writing so that Timothy will know how it is necessary to conduct himself in the household of God" (Tomlinson, "Pastoral Epistles," 60). According to Trebilco (*Ephesus*, 562), "the ethos and ordering of the church should reflect the values and ethos of the traditional household of the time."

11. According to Goodwin (*Apostle of the Living God*, 86), "early Christian Gentile communities, like those addressed in Paul's letters, came to be defined as communities whose identity was grounded in monotheistic worship, that is, the worship of the living God. These communities were aptly named 'temples' or 'churches' of the living God (2 Cor 6:16; 1 Tim 3:15), since they distinguished themselves in a pagan environment by their exclusive commitment to the living God."

mystery of godliness. It stands in stunning contrast to the "great" god-dess Artemis, whose temple and center of worship was in Ephesus. According to the Acts of the Apostles, during the riot in the theater at Ephesus the Ephesians shouted in unison for about two hours, "Great (*megalē*) is Artemis of the Ephesians!" (Acts 19:28; 34–35).[12]

This great mystery of godliness that Paul leads his audience to con-fess functions as doxological worship in praise of God for the salvific activity he has accomplished in the Christ event.[13] This great mystery of godliness is expressed as a liturgical hymn artistically arranged in three poetic couplets succinctly summarizing the christological history of salvation in a chiastic pattern alternating between events on earth and in heaven (3:16b). The hymn praises God for the Christ who (a) was manifested in the flesh (earth), (b) was vindicated in the Spirit (heaven), (b) was seen by angels (heaven), (a) was proclaimed among Gentiles (earth), (a) was believed in the world (earth), (b) was taken up in glory (heaven).[14]

All of the activity proclaimed in this hymn has its ultimate source in God. All of the verbs can be understood as divine passives. Thus, the hymn praises God for the Christ whom God manifested in the flesh during his earthly existence, but vindicated by raising him from the dead to a heavenly existence in the Spirit. It praises God for raising the Christ from the dead so that he could be seen by angels in heaven, and for inspiring people on earth to proclaim the risen Christ among the Gentiles. It praises God for granting the faith by which Christ was believed in the world on earth, and for taking up and thus exalting Christ in glory in heaven. By confessing this hymn as the great mystery of godliness, the audience praise God for the missionary activity that advances the salvation of all, a major theme of the letter.[15]

12. On Artemis of Ephesus, see Trebilco, *Ephesus*, 19–30. "Given the Ephesian set-ting, whether or not the famous riot associated with Paul's ministry (Acts 19) was still fresh in mind, it is impossible not to hear in Paul's statement a subversive echo of the city's bold claim, 'Great is Artemis of the Ephesians' (Acts 19:28, 34; cf. 19:27, 35)" (Towner, *Timothy and Titus*, 277).

13. Akin, "Pastoral Epistles," 137–52.

14. "The hymn consists of three sets of couplets. The rationale behind this arrange-ment can be understood in various ways. Much the most widely accepted analysis finds three contrasting couplets with a chiastic arrangement of statements giving an alternation between earth and heaven" (Marshall, *Pastoral Epistles*, 501).

15. "The Christ hymn (v. 16b) now introduced is the rhetorical and christologi-

Timothy as a Model Teacher regarding Worship

Part of the false teaching includes abstaining from certain foods (4:3a). But, as a model teacher regarding matters of worship, Timothy is to point out to the believers at Ephesus how they are to respond to this false teaching with an authentic worship of God, which includes prayers of thanksgiving for what God has created as beneficial. Timothy is to point out that these foods need not be avoided, since God created them "for sharing with thanksgiving by those who believe and know the truth, for every creature of God is commendable and nothing is to be rejected when received with thanksgiving, for it is made holy through the word of God and prayer" (4:3b-5).[16]

Timothy is to discipline himself for the "godliness" (*eusebeia*) that includes both liturgical and ethical worship (4:7). Such godliness has a promise of life, whose source is the living God (3:15), for the present and for the future (4:8). Indeed, we believers have hoped upon the living God, who is savior of all human beings, especially of those who believe (4:10).[17] And Timothy is to "become a model for those who believe, in word, in conduct, in love, in faith, in purity" (4:12), or, in other words, in godliness.

Until Paul arrives Timothy is to exercise his authoritative role as leader of worship in the liturgical assembly. He is to attend to the public reading of the scriptures, to preaching the exhortation inspired by

---

cal high point of the letter. It expresses a very strongly missiological interpretation of Christian existence that draws its meaning from a Christianity that stresses the humanity of Christ. Both these dimensions are perfectly consonant with the christological and missiological themes of the letter already under construction (1:15; 2:1-7). These themes both point to and emanate from the central confession of 'the mystery of godliness'" (Towner, *Timothy and Titus*, 276).

16. "'Thanksgiving' in 4:3-4, associated with table prayer elsewhere in Paul (1 Cor 10:30), is the acknowledgment of God as the creative source of the gift of food. Possibly in this context 'prayer' ('intercession') should be understood as a generic term for prayer not to be rigidly distinguished from 'thanksgiving.' In any case, the function of prayer is to acknowledge consciously God's provision and his people's acceptance of the gift of food in the awareness of his presence and in fellowship with other believers" (ibid., 299). See also Johnson, *Letters to Timothy*, 242.

17. Goodwin, "1 Timothy 4.10," 65-85; idem, *Apostle of the Living God*, 138-39; "Reference to 'the living God' calls forth a specifically salvation-oriented description of God and his will to save people. The designation of God as 'Savior' is thematic in this letter (see 1:1; 2:3)" (Towner, *Timothy and Titus*, 310).

them, and to teaching the doctrine based on them (4:13).[18] Timothy is not to neglect the gift given to him as a result of prophecies when the hands of the presbyterate were imposed upon him, authorizing and equipping him for his role of leadership (4:14).[19] He is to take care of and be absorbed in these matters regarding communal worship, so that his progress may be manifest as a model to all (4:15). By holding fast to the task of the teaching of the doctrine, he will save both himself and those who listen to him, as they are gathered together within the worshiping assembly (4:16).

Worship in the Household

Within the household of believers children or grandchildren are to extend godliness to their widowed mother or grandmother by financially supporting her, for this is "acceptable" (*apodekton*) before God (5:4). It thus amounts to the godliness of "acceptable" ethical worship of God (cf. 2:3).[20] The real widow, on the other hand, who has been left alone without any family members to support her, has hoped upon God and remains in petitions and prayers night and day (5:5). She thus engages in the liturgical worship of praying to the living God (cf. 4:10) for her livelihood. In contrast to the self-indulgent widow who, even while living, has died (5:6), the real widow, through her continual petitions and prayers, is focused on the new life provided by the living God.

Worship in the Letter's Closing

As the letter comes to a close, Paul commands before the God who gives life to all (6:13) that Timothy keep all that Paul has commanded him to do in Ephesus, faultlessly irreproachable until the final appearance of our Lord Jesus Christ (6:14). Paul then leads Timothy and the Ephesian congregation in an act of doxological worship that praises God as the blessed and only sovereign who will manifest this final appearance of

18. Towner, "1 Tim 4:13," 44–54; Wolfe, "Sagacious Use of Scripture," 199–218.

19. Tipei, *Laying on of Hands*, 262–71.

20. "On the model of the 'acceptable' sacrifice from Leviticus, the care of the family members for older relatives is behavior that accords with God's will" (Towner, *Timothy and Titus*, 340).

our Lord Jesus Christ (6:15a). He goes on to praise God as "the King of those reigning and the Lord of those ruling, the only one having immortality, dwelling in unapproachable light, whom no one from human beings has seen or is able to see, to whom be honor and eternal might. Amen!" (6:15b–16). The audience are invited to join in and affirm this doxological worship by adding their own reverberating "Amen!"[21]

After a final exhortation to Timothy to guard what has been entrusted to him (6:20), Paul closes the letter with a final prayer-greeting, "Grace with you!" (6:21). The "you" (*hymōn*) here is the plural pronoun, so that the prayer is not only for Timothy but for the entire Ephesian audience. With this final greeting Paul not only acknowledges and affirms the divine grace the audience have already received, but prays that, as a result of having listened to the letter, they may continue to experience the divine grace that super-abounded for Paul (1:14). This final prayer-greeting for "grace" thus forms a literary inclusion with the opening prayer-greeting addressed to Timothy for "grace," mercy, and peace from God the Father and Christ Jesus our Lord (1:2), and thus completes the worship framework that envelopes the entire letter.[22]

Conclusion: Worship in 1 Timothy

At the beginning of the letter, after addressing Timothy as "a genuine child in faith," Paul pronounces the initial ritualistic greeting, praying that through the letter not only Timothy (1:1–2a) but the entire

21. "All that is left after so majestic a litany is an expression of doxology uttered in awe. This doxology takes the standard form, with the relative pronoun ('to whom') drawing the recipient of praise ('him') from the preceding statement. This confession of God's 'honor' repeats the earlier doxology (see on 1:17). Here it is linked with his 'might,' which was typically attributed to God in Jewish and Christian thought. The ascription is strengthened by extending the validity of the claim to eternity. And the 'Amen' invites the agreement of Timothy and the Ephesian church" (ibid., 422–23).

22. According to Towner (ibid., 435), this final prayer-greeting "is a serious and caring prayer of the apostle that Timothy and those to whom he was sent (pl. 'you') would experience God's gracious presence among them. . . . But the wider scope of the blessing corresponds to the adaptation of mandate elements in the crafting of a letter written to Timothy and secondarily to the church receiving him. When one draws together the opening blessing of Timothy (1:2) and this closing benediction, it becomes apparent that Paul views his coworker's task and this church's life as equally carried out within the protective and nurturing grace of God. Paul's closing prayer-wish is that they will work and live in full awareness of the Lord's real presence among them."

Christian community in Ephesus (1:3) may be the recipients of grace, mercy, and peace from God the Father and Christ Jesus "our" Lord (1:2b)—the Lord of all believers. Paul brings the confession that he is the prototypical recipient of divine mercy as a sinner (1:15–16) to a climax as he leads his audience to join him in a stirring act of doxological worship: "To the king of the ages, immortal, invisible, the only God, honor and glory to the ages of the ages. Amen!" (1:17).

Paul's first letter to Timothy abounds with instructions for the "godliness" that embraces both liturgical and ethical worship. Men are to be "purified" for proper liturgical worship by making sure that their ethical conduct is free of anger and disputes (2:8), in contrast to the divisiveness of the false teachers (1:3). Timothy is to instruct the women, the wives of the men, that the virtues of modesty and prudence in their attire are appropriate for their proper liturgical worship. And they are to be engaged in the doing of good works for their proper ethical worship, in accord with their professed claim of "reverence to God" (2:9–10). All those who minister commendably in the community, including the services they perform for the worship of the assembly, obtain much publicity that attracts people to faith in Christ Jesus, and thus play their role in advancing the cause of universal salvation (3:13).

Although absent, Paul, through the letter as a substitute for his personal presence, leads Timothy and the community in an act of hymnic worship of the living God that confesses "the great mystery of godliness." The poetically patterned hymn (3:16) praises God for the Christ who (a) was manifested in the flesh (earth), (b) was vindicated in the Spirit (heaven), (b) was seen by angels (heaven), (a) was proclaimed among Gentiles (earth), (a) was believed in the world (earth), (b) was taken up in glory (heaven). By confessing this hymn as the great mystery of godliness, the audience praise God for the missionary activity that advances the salvation of all, a major theme of the letter.

Until Paul arrives Timothy is to be a model of godliness in the exercise of his authoritative role as leader of worship in the liturgical assembly. He is to attend to the public reading of the scriptures, to preaching the exhortation inspired by them, and to teaching the doctrine based on them (4:13). Timothy is not to neglect the gift given to him as a result of prophecies when the hands of the presbyterate were imposed upon him, authorizing and equipping him for his role of leadership (4:14). He is to take care of and be absorbed in these matters regarding communal worship, so that his progress may be manifest as a model to all (4:15). By holding fast to the task of the teaching of the doctrine, he will save both himself and those who listen to him, as they are gathered together within the worshiping assembly (4:16).

Within the household of believers children or grandchildren are to perform acceptable ethical worship of God by financially supporting their widowed mother or grandmother (5:4). In contrast to the self-indulgent widow who, even while living, has died (5:6), the real widow who has no family members to support her, through her continual petitions and prayers, is focused on the new life provided by the living God (5:5).

As the letter comes to a close, Paul leads Timothy and the Ephesian congregation in an act of doxological worship that praises God as "the King of those reigning and the Lord of those ruling, the only one having immortality, dwelling in unapproachable light, whom no one from human beings has seen or is able to see, to whom be honor and eternal might. Amen!" (6:15–16). Paul's final prayer-greeting of "grace with you!" (6:21) not only acknowledges and affirms the divine grace the audience have already received, but prays that, as a result of having listened to the letter, they may continue to experience the divine grace that superabounded for Paul (1:14). This final prayer-greeting for "grace" forms a literary inclusion with the opening prayer-greeting addressed to Timothy for "grace," mercy, and peace from God the Father and Christ Jesus our Lord (1:2), and thus completes the framework of worship that not only envelopes but permeates Paul's first letter to Timothy.

2 Timothy

Paul is imprisoned in Rome (2 Tim 1:16–17; 2:9) when he sends the second letter to Timothy, his delegate in Ephesus (1:18; 4:12). Apparently Paul was released from his earlier imprisonment in Rome, the one that seems to correspond to that mentioned in Acts 28:16–31 and during which he most likely sent his letter to the Philippians. According to that letter, Paul indeed expected to be released and planned to come to Philippi (Phil 1:24–25; 2:24). But Paul evidently was eventually arrested again, probably at Troas (2 Tim 4:13), and imprisoned for a second time in Rome. Although many consider this letter to be Paul's farewell or last will and testament, a close reading of the text indicates that this is questionable, or at least in need of a more nuanced interpretation. While Paul is certainly aware of the very real possibility that he will be executed during this imprisonment (and, in accord with a prevalent tradition regarding his martyrdom in Rome, this may well have been the case), he nevertheless hopes to be freed soon for further ministry with Timothy, who is to return from Ephesus to join Paul (4:9–13).[1]

In accord with Paul's prophecy at Miletus to the presbyters of Ephesus in Acts 20:29–31, the situation of the church in Ephesus has grown worse over time, and Timothy finds himself in the midst of it. Paul charges Timothy, as his delegate, to persevere in preaching, teaching, and evangelizing by following the model of ministry exemplified by Paul himself, even and especially during Paul's current trial and imprisonment (2 Tim 4:1–8). Timothy is to come to Rome soon, before winter if possible (4:21) but after the arrival of Tychicus, whom Paul sent to Ephesus apparently to replace Timothy (4:12). Paul wants Timothy, his

---

1. Smith, *Timothy's Task*, 226–28. See also Prior, *Paul the Letter-Writer*; Murphy-O'Connor, "2 Timothy," 403–18.

long-time companion and dependable coworker, to join him so that they can continue the mission of preaching the gospel together after Paul's hoped-for release from prison (4:9–17).[2] As in the case of Paul's other letters to delegates, the letters of Titus and 1 Timothy, he indirectly addresses the liturgical assembly by directly addressing the delegate, in this case Timothy. This establishes a rhetorical strategy that enhances the authority of the delegate within the community, and it provides the community with criteria for holding the delegate responsible for carrying out Paul's instructions to him.

2 Timothy as a Ritual of Worship

Introductory Worship

Although Paul addresses the letter to "Timothy, a beloved child" (1:2a), his initial ritualistic prayer-greeting of "grace, mercy, peace from God the Father and Christ Jesus our Lord" (1:2b) indicates a communal dimension with its reference to "our" Lord—the Lord not only of Paul and Timothy but of the letter's Ephesian audience. Then, continuing the letter's worship dimension with his own response of worship to the "grace," the *charis* that comes from God, Paul declares that "I have thanks," literally, "I have grace," that is, *charis*, "for God, whom I worship [cf. Rom 1:9] as my ancestors did in a clean conscience, as I have constant memory concerning you in my prayers night and day" (1:3). The "grace" that comes from God inspires Paul to have the "grace" that renders gratitude and praise to the God whom Paul worships and to whom his continual prayers for Timothy are directed. Paul's gratitude and praise for the God whom "I worship" (*latreuō*) as did his Jewish ancestors aligns his worship with that of Timothy's immediate Jewish ancestors, namely, his grandmother Lois and his mother Eunice, from whom Timothy inherited his faith in God (1:5). Paul's assurance to Timothy of his continual remembrance of him in his prayers is embraced by this worship.

---

2. "2 Timothy is certainly not a farewell letter or last will and testament since Paul is hopeful that he will be released soon to continue his ministry. Rather this is a paraenetic letter written to encourage Timothy to continue to stand firm as a minister and to continue in suffering for the Gospel with Paul" (Smith, *Timothy's Task*, 228).

Paul further explains this grace that motivates not only his own worship, but the worship of Timothy, the Ephesian audience, and all believers. The communal dimension of this worship is evident and underlined by his use of several inclusive first-person plural pronouns when he describes the gospel for which he is suffering imprisonment. It is the gospel that accords, as he declares, "to the power of God, who saved *us* and called *us* with a holy calling, not according to *our* works but according to his own purpose and grace, which was granted to *us* in Christ Jesus before eternal times, but manifested now through the appearance of *our* savior Christ Jesus, who abolished death but enlightened life and immortality through the gospel" (1:8–9).[3]

As in the case of his first letter to Timothy (1 Tim 1:2), Paul adds "mercy" (*eleos*) to the usual grace and peace mentioned in the initial prayer-greeting of this second letter to Timothy (2 Tim 1:2). Paul elaborates this distinctive divine "mercy" when he performs another act of epistolary worship, praying for noteworthy members of the liturgical assembly in Ephesus: "May the Lord grant mercy (*eleos*) to the household of Onesiphorus, because many times he refreshed me and was not ashamed of my chain, but being in Rome, he diligently searched for and found me. May the Lord grant him to find mercy (*eleos*) from the Lord on that day" (1:16–18).[4]

Worship in the Body of the Letter

Paul indicates the implications of the divine "grace" he prayed for from God the Father and Christ Jesus our Lord in the initial prayer-greeting (1:2) when he prayerfully urges Timothy, "You then, my child, be empowered in the grace that is in Christ Jesus, and the things you heard from me through many witnesses, these things deposit to faithful people, who will be competent to teach others" (2:1–2). And Paul further motivates the worship of the community with the following hymnic

3. On the theme of salvation in 2 Timothy, see Wieland, *Significance of Salvation*, 109–79.

4. "As in Paul's other wish-prayers (v. 18a), the wish is intended as a prayer expressed indirectly to the Lord (Jesus) but directly to the one or ones to be blessed, showing a sense of solidarity and immediacy of concern. This specific wish for mercy to be granted is rooted in the OT understanding of God's desire to help his people" (Towner, *Timothy and Titus*, 482).

proclamation by which he leads the liturgical assembly in a communal celebration of the gracious faithfulness of Jesus Christ: "For if we have died with him, we will also live with him. If we endure, we will also reign with him. If we deny him, he will also deny us. If we are unfaithful, he remains faithful, for he is not able to deny himself" (2:11–13). The surprising twist at the conclusion of this hymn in praise of divine grace, namely, that he remains faithful even if we are unfaithful, for he is not able to deny himself, resonates with the marvelously gracious "righteousness of God" that Paul referred to in previous letters (cf. Rom 1:17), and exemplifies the divine saving "grace" that inspires and motivates worship.

Paul assures his audience that, in contrast to false teaching (2:16–18), the solid foundation of God remains standing in accord with the scriptural confirmation from Num 16:5 that "the Lord knows those who are his," and the scriptural exhortation recalling Sir 17:26 and Lev 24:16, "Let withdraw from wrongdoing everyone who names the name of the Lord" (2 Tim 2:19). These two scriptural sayings provide another indication of the close relationship between liturgical and ethical worship. Everyone who names the name of the Lord in communal worship must also withdraw from the wrongdoing of false teaching in order to complement liturgical worship with proper ethical worship.[5] Paul goes on to point out that if someone cleanses himself from the things associated with false teaching, he will be a "vessel" in the large household (2:20), alluding to the household which is the church that worships God, "for honor, sanctified, useful to the master, prepared for every good work" (2:21). In other words, believers must separate themselves from false teaching as those made holy by and for God, prepared for every good work that renders ethical worship to God.

Timothy is to be not only a participating member but also a leader within the worshiping assembly. He is to "pursue righteousness, faith, love, and peace with those who call upon the Lord from a clean heart" (2:22), that is, with those who call upon the Lord in communal worship. He is not to be involved in quarrels, but, as a leader, he should be able to teach (2:23–24), "in kindness correcting the opponents, that

---

5. "This passage is an excellent example of the intimate connection within these epistles between right believing and right living. The first saying addresses the doctrinal issue, and the second sets forth the practical imperative based upon the doctrinal indicative" (Wolfe, "Sagacious Use of Scripture," 204).

God may perhaps grant them repentance for knowledge of the truth" (2:25). Paul warns Timothy, and thus the Ephesian community, "all who are willing to live godly in Christ Jesus will be persecuted" (3:12). But Timothy is to remain in the things he learned from his infancy, which include the "sacred writings." They are able to give him, and by implication every believer, wisdom for salvation through the faith that is in Christ Jesus (3:14–15). Paul points out the benefit of the sacred scriptures proclaimed in the liturgical assembly for the teaching that is part of worship when he declares, "All scripture is inspired by God and advantageous for doctrine, for reproof, for correction, for training in righteousness, that the person of God may be proficient, equipped for every good work" (3:16–17). The scripture one hears in liturgical worship equips worshipers for the good work of ethical worship.

Paul then, "before God and Christ Jesus," solemnly charges Timothy (4:1), equipped with the sacred scriptures, to play his leadership role as teacher within the liturgical assembly. Timothy is to "preach the word, be ready whether it is convenient or inconvenient, reprove, rebuke, exhort in all patience and teaching" (4:2). The sacred scriptures proclaimed in the liturgical assembly will thus empower Timothy to deal effectively with whatever false teaching arises (4:3–4). With the aid of the sacred scriptures Timothy is to suffer hardship, do the work of an evangelist, and fulfill his ministry (4:5), a ministry that includes teaching within the liturgical assembly, so that the believing community in Ephesus may offer proper liturgical and ethical worship to God.

Worship in the Letter's Closing

As the letter begins to come to a close, Paul offers himself and his own situation as a model not only for Timothy but also for all believers. When Paul declares that "I myself am already being poured out" (4:6a), he employs the cultic image of a sacrificial drink offering to describe the ordeal of his preaching the gospel during the trials of his imprisonment and his potential execution as a form of worship offered to God. Paul is convinced that the time of his "release" (*analyseōs*), that is, his release from imprisonment, whether through death by being executed or through dismissal by being acquitted, is at hand (4:6b). Either way, Paul boldly proclaims that he fought the "commendable fight," the fight that is "commendable" (*kalon*) both to God and human beings, the fight that amounts to an ethical worship of praise to God and leads others to offer praise to God (4:7). Whether Paul is released from prison by being executed or by being acquitted, he looks forward to the eternal reward that he and all believers can expect for their ethical worship: "henceforth the crown of righteousness is reserved for me, which the Lord, the just judge, will repay to me on that day, and not only to me but to all who have loved his appearance" (4:8).

Paul's personal worship of praise for the grace that has already and will further empower him provides a model for Timothy and all believers, as he leads his audience in an act of doxological worship: "But the Lord stood by me and empowered me, that through me the proclamation might be fulfilled, and all the Gentiles might hear, and I was rescued from the mouth of the lion. The Lord will rescue me from every evil work and will save me in his heavenly kingdom, to whom be glory to the ages of the ages. Amen!" (4:17–18). The Ephesian worshiping community is invited to join Paul in his doxological worship by adding their own assenting, affirmative, and reverberating "Amen!"[6]

All of the dimensions of the "grace" elaborated in the letter are summed up by Paul's climactic final prayer-greeting. After the greeting addressed to Timothy alone, "the Lord with your (singular) spirit" (4:22a), Paul addresses not only Timothy but the entire liturgical assembly with the final, climactic greeting, "the grace with you (plural)" (4:22b). Paul thus prays that *the* "grace" that they have already received and that is still with them continue to be with them after and as a result of listening to the letter. This final greeting of "grace" forms a literary inclusion with the opening greeting of "grace" (1:2) to envelope the entire letter within a context of prayerful worship. This is *the* "grace" that

---

6. "Some commentators are of the opinion that the doxology is offered to God (as in 1 Tim 1:17), but while it is something of a departure from Pauline practice, the relative pronoun 'to whom' has the Lord (Jesus) as its most obvious antecedent (cf. 1 Tim 1:12). By means of the doxology, Paul affirms strongly that the majesty and dominion (to which 'glory' refers) are proper to the Lord. The concluding 'Amen' punctuates the affirmation as an undeniable fact to which he is completely committed. As a conclusion to the body of the letter, the doxology invites readers to add their voice to Paul's worship" (Towner, *Timothy and Titus*, 648).

inspires and motivates the worship not only of Paul, Timothy, and the church at Ephesus, but of all believers.[7]

Conclusion: Worship in 2 Timothy

The "grace" that comes from God inspires Paul to have the "grace" that renders gratitude and praise to the God whom Paul worships and to whom his continual prayers for Timothy are directed (1:2–3). The communal dimension of this worship is evident and underlined by his use of several inclusive first-person plural pronouns when he describes the gospel for which he is suffering imprisonment (1:8–9). Paul elaborates the distinctive divine "mercy," which he has added to the usual initial prayer-greeting of grace and peace (1:2), when he performs another act of epistolary worship, praying that God may grant noteworthy members of the liturgical assembly in Ephesus the gift of this mercy (1:16–18).

The surprising twist at the conclusion of the hymn that celebrates the gracious faithfulness of Jesus Christ (2:11–13), namely, that he remains faithful even if we are unfaithful, for he is not able to deny himself, exemplifies the divine grace that inspires and motivates worship. Everyone who names the name of the Lord in communal worship must also withdraw from the wrongdoing of false teaching in order to complement liturgical worship with proper ethical worship (2:19). Paul points out the benefit of the sacred scriptures proclaimed in the liturgical assembly for the teaching that is part of communal worship. The scripture one hears in liturgical worship equips him or her for the good work of ethical worship (3:16–17). The sacred scriptures proclaimed in the liturgical assembly will empower Timothy to deal effectively with whatever false teaching arises (4:3–4). With the aid of the sacred scriptures Timothy is to suffer hardship, do the work of an evangelist, and fulfill his ministry (4:5), a ministry that includes teaching within the

7. "The grace wish is a genuine prayer for the Lord's gracious presence in the lives of the recipients; it is directed toward a broader group (pl. 'you'). The shift to the plural may be accounted for partly by those previously mentioned (4:19) with whom Timothy is to communicate Paul's greetings, and partly by those of the church who would hear the letter read (as in the case of 1 Timothy). In form it duplicates the benedictions of 1 Tim 6:21 and Col 4:18 (cf. Heb 13:25), which also omit explicit reference to the divine source of grace, though the implicit meaning is obvious. . . . His benedictions to his churches and coworkers were serious expressions of prayer for his people, that they might know the Lord's presence and help in all situations" (ibid., 655–56).

liturgical assembly, so that the believers in Ephesus may offer proper liturgical and ethical worship to God.

When Paul declares that "I myself am already being poured out" (4:6a), he employs the cultic image of a sacrificial drink offering to describe the ordeal of his preaching the gospel during the trials of his imprisonment and his potential execution as a form of worship offered to God. Whether Paul is released from prison by being executed or by being acquitted, he looks forward to the eternal reward that he and all believers can expect for their ethical worship (4:6b-8). Paul's personal worship of praise for the grace that has already and will further empower him provides a model for Timothy and all believers, as he leads his audience in an act of doxological worship to which they are invited to join Paul by adding their own reverberating "Amen!" (4:17–18). With the final, climactic greeting, "the grace with you (plural)" (4:22b), Paul prays that *the* "grace" that Timothy and the Ephesian community have already received and that is still with them continue to be with them after and as a result of listening to the letter. This final greeting of "grace" forms a literary inclusion with the opening greeting of "grace" (1:2) to envelope the entire letter within a context of prayerful worship. This is *the* "grace" that inspires and motivates both the liturgical and ethical worship not only of Paul, Timothy, and the church at Ephesus, but of all believers.

Conclusion
The Letters of Paul as Rituals of Worship

Detailed summaries of each of the thirteen letters of Paul as rituals of worship can be found at the end of each of the preceding thirteen chapters. Although each of the letters can be considered as a ritual of worship, each exhibits its own distinct and unique elements in that regard. Hence I have decided not to attempt to harmonize or synthesize the letters from the point of view of the worship themes they project. Indeed, each letter should be appreciated as a unique Pauline ritual of worship.

Nevertheless, there are some key points common to all of the letters as rituals of worship, which can be briefly presented in this concluding chapter. First of all, despite the rich diversity of content in these letters, and despite disputes about the Pauline authorship of several of them, it is most noteworthy that all thirteen of the letters of Paul begin and end with a prayer-greeting for divine grace. The literary inclusions formed by these prayer-greetings for grace thus enclose each of the letters within a context of prayerful worship.

The divine grace that Paul prays for on behalf of his audiences in these prayer-greetings refers in a comprehensive, but succinctly and abbreviated way, to the saving grace that God the Father freely gives as a result of the salvation accomplished in and through the life, death, and resurrection of his Son, the Lord Jesus Christ. This term "grace" thus epitomizes the divine, definitive salvation now available to all who accept it through faith. It is this saving grace that inspires, motivates, and empowers the worship in these letters.

Secondly, each of the letters includes ritualistic, liturgical language, such as, prayers, petitions, thanksgivings, benedictions, and doxologies. Paul prays for his audiences and requests their prayers for him.

As the epistolary presider of the worship for which his audiences are gathered as a community to listen to his letters, Paul leads them in worship by performing various acts of epistolary worship within the letters themselves, often inviting their reverberating "Amen!"—their ritualistic affirmation and assent as a liturgical assembly. The ritualistic language of these letters thus enhances their dimension as liturgical homilies or sermons heard by their audiences as worshiping assemblies.

Thirdly, each of the letters refers to the ethical or moral worship of the audiences that complements their liturgical worship. Inspired and empowered by their liturgical worship, believers are to conduct their lives in a way that amounts to offering worship that praises and glorifies God. Paul often employs sacrificial, cultic terms, such as, "holy, blameless, and unblemished," to characterize the moral lives of his audiences as sacrificial worship that is most pleasing and acceptable before God.

In short, in and through all of his letters the apostle Paul presents himself as the preeminent and paradigmatic person of prayer and worship—both liturgical and ethical worship. At climactic turning points in his remarkable missionary career, Paul models for us some very magnificent, majestic, and memorable prayers. As speech acts, they accomplish what they say and exert a profound effect on us in our very hearing of them. At the end of his letter to the Romans, the most comprehensive presentation of his gospel, as he contemplates his journey to Jerusalem and looks forward to visiting the Roman believers on his way to further missionary activity in Spain, Paul leads his audience to join him in a very powerful prayer of praise that glorifies the God of gracious power:

> To him who has the power to strengthen you according to my gospel and the preaching of Jesus Christ, according to the revelation of the mystery kept secret for long ages, but now manifested and made known through the prophetic writings in accord with the command of the eternal God for the obedience of faith among all the nations—to the only wise God, through Jesus Christ, glory forever! Amen! (Rom 16:25–27)

At the end of the first half of his letter to the Ephesians, in which Paul, while he sits in prison, has presented the mystically awesome cosmic mystery of the divine power at work in Christ and the church, he leads his audience to join him in a sublimely inspiring prayer of praise that glorifies the God of gracious power:

> Now to him who has the power to do far more beyond all that we ask or imagine according to the power that is working in us, to him be glory in the church and in Christ Jesus to all the generations, for ever and ever. Amen!" (Eph 3:20–21)

And finally, at the end of his second letter to Timothy, the imprisoned Paul sums up his experience of the grace of God in terms of the power of God operative throughout his apostolic ministry, as he leads his audience to join him in a hope-filled prayer of praise that glorifies the God of gracious power:

> But the Lord stood by me and empowered me, that through me the proclamation might be fulfilled, and all the Gentiles might hear, and I was rescued from the mouth of the lion. The Lord will rescue me from every evil work and will save me in his heavenly kingdom, to whom be glory to the ages of the ages. Amen!" (2 Tim 4:17–18)

Bibliography

Abernathy, David. "Paul's Thorn in the Flesh: A Messenger of Satan?" *Neot* 35 (2001) 69–79.

Adewuya, J. Ayodeji. *Holiness and Community in 2 Cor. 6:14–7:1: Paul's View of Communal Holiness in the Corinthian Correspondence.* Studies in Biblical Literature 40. New York: Lang, 2001.

———. "The People of God in a Pluralistic Society: Holiness in 2 Corinthians." In *Holiness and Ecclesiology in the New Testament,* edited by Kent E. Brower and Andy Johnson, 201–18. Grand Rapids: Eerdmans, 2007.

Akin, Daniel L. "The Mystery of Godliness Is Great: Christology in the Pastoral Epistles." In *Entrusted with the Gospel: Paul's Theology in the Pastoral Epistles,* edited by Andreas J. Köstenberger and Terry L. Wilder, 137–52. Nashville: Broadman & Holman, 2010.

Arichea, D. C. "Who Was Phoebe? Translating *Diakonos* in Romans 16.1." *BT* 39 (1988) 401–9.

Ascough, Richard S. "The Completion of a Religious Duty: The Background of 2 Cor 8.1–15." *NTS* 42 (1996) 584–99.

———. *Paul's Macedonian Associations: The Social Context of Philippians and 1 Thessalonians.* WUNT 161. Tübingen: Mohr/Siebeck, 2003.

———. "Thessalonians, First Letter to the." In *The New Interpreter's Dictionary of the Bible,* 5:569–74. Nashville: Abingdon, 2009.

———. "Thessalonians, Second Letter to the." In *The New Interpreter's Dictionary of the Bible,* 5:574–79. Nashville: Abingdon, 2009.

Aus, Roger David. "The Liturgical Background of the Necessity and Propriety of Giving Thanks According to 2 Thess 1:3." *JBL* 92 (1973) 432–38.

Austin, John Langshaw. *How to Do Things with Words.* Cambridge, MA: Harvard University Press, 1962.

Bailey, J. L. "Perspectives from Prison: Reading Philippians." *Trinity Seminary Review* 27 (2006) 83–97.

Balch, David L. "Rich Pompeiian Houses, Shops for Rent, and the Huge Apartment Building in Herculaneum as Typical Spaces for Pauline House Churches." *JSNT* 27 (2004) 27–46.

Balz, Horst. "*euchomai.*" In *EDNT* 2:88–89.

———. "*hosios.*" In *EDNT* 2:536–37.

———. "*leitourgia.*" In *EDNT* 2:347–49.

Banks, Robert J. "Romans 7:25a: An Eschatologial Thanksgiving?" *ABR* 26 (1978) 34–42.

Barr, James. "'*Abba* Isn't Daddy." *JTS* 39 (1988) 28–47.

Batten, Alicia J. "Neither Gold nor Braided Hair (1 Timothy 2.9; 1 Peter 3.3): Adornment, Gender and Honour in Antiquity." *NTS* 55 (2009) 484–501.

Beetham, Christopher A. *Echoes of Scripture in the Letter of Paul to the Colossians*. BIS 96. Leiden: Brill, 2008.

Beutler, Johannes. "*martys*." In *EDNT* 2:393–95.

Bevere, Allan R. *Sharing in the Inheritance: Identity and the Moral Life in Colossians*. JSNTSup 226. London: Sheffield Academic, 2003.

Bittlinger, A. *Gifts and Graces*. London: Hodder and Stoughton, 1967.

Blackwell, Ben C. "Immortal Glory and the Problem of Death in Romans 3.23." *JSNT* 32 (2010) 285–308.

Blomberg, Craig L. *From Pentecost to Patmos: An Introduction to Acts through Revelation*. Nashville: Broadman & Holman, 2006.

Bockmuehl, Markus N. A. *The Epistle to the Philippians*. BNTC 11. Peabody, MA: Hendrickson, 1998.

Boer, Martinus C., de. *The Defeat of Death: Apocalyptic Eschatology in 1 Corinthians 15 and Romans 5*. JSNTSup 22. Sheffield: JSOT, 1988.

Borchert, Gerald L. *Worship in the New Testament: Divine Mystery and Human Response*. St. Louis: Chalice, 2008.

Bormann, Lukas. *Philippi: Stadt und Christengemeinde zur Zeit des Paulus*. NovTSup 78. Leiden: Brill, 1995.

Bruce, Frederick Fyvie. *The Epistle to the Galatians*. NIGTC. Grand Rapids: Eerdmans, 1982.

Burke, Trevor J. *Adopted into God's Family: Exploring a Pauline Metaphor*. New Studies in Biblical Theology 22. Downers Grove, IL: InterVarsity, 2006.

Burridge, Richard A. *Imitating Jesus: An Inclusive Approach to New Testament Ethics*. Grand Rapids: Eerdmans, 2007.

Burton, Ernest De Witt. *A Critical and Exegetical Commentary on the Epistle to the Galatians*. New York: Charles Scribner's Sons, 1920.

Byrne, Brendan. *Romans*. SP 6. Collegeville, MN: Liturgical, 1996.

Carson, Donald A., and Douglas J. Moo. *An Introduction to the New Testament*. Grand Rapids: Zondervan, 2005.

Cassidy, Richard J. *Four Times Peter: Portrayals of Peter in the Four Gospels and at Philippi*. Collegeville, MN: Liturgical, 2007.

———. *Paul in Chains: Roman Imprisonment and the Letters of St. Paul*. New York: Crossroad, 2001.

Cohick, Lynn H. *Women in the World of the Earliest Christians: Illuminating Ancient Ways of Life*. Grand Rapids: Baker, 2009.

Collins, Raymond F. *First Corinthians*. SP 7. Collegeville, MN: Liturgical, 1999.

Couser, Greg A. "The Sovereign Savior of 1 and 2 Timothy and Titus." In *Entrusted with the Gospel: Paul's Theology in the Pastoral Epistles*, edited by Andreas J. Köstenberger and Terry L. Wilder, 105–36. Nashville: Broadman & Holman, 2010.

DeMaris, Richard E. *The New Testament in Its Ritual World*. London: Routledge, 2008.

Donfried, Karl Paul. "Rethinking Scholarly Approaches to 1 Timothy." In *1 Timothy Reconsidered*, edited by Karl Paul Donfried, 153–82. Colloquium Oecumenicum Paulinum 18. Leuven: Peeters, 2008.

Dunn, James D. G. "The Colossian Philosophy: A Confident Jewish Apologia." *Bib* 76 (1995) 153–81.

———. *The Epistles to the Colossians and to Philemon*. NIGTC. Grand Rapids: Eerdmans, 1996.

———. *The Theology of Paul the Apostle*. Grand Rapids: Eerdmans, 1998.

Eastman, Brad. *The Significance of Grace in the Letters of Paul*. Studies in Biblical Literature 11. New York: Lang, 1999.

Ellis, E. Earle. *History and Interpretation in New Testament Perspective*. BIS 54. Atlanta: Society of Biblical Literature, 2001.

———. *The Making of the New Testament Documents*. Leiden: Brill, 2002.

Farkasfalvy, Denis. "The Eucharistic Provenance of New Testament Texts." In *Rediscovering the Eucharist: Ecumenical Conversations*, edited by Roch A. Kereszty, 27–51. Mahwah, NJ: Paulist, 2003.

Fee, Gordon D. *The First Epistle to the Corinthians*. NICNT. Grand Rapids: Eerdmans, 1987.

———. *The First and Second Letters to the Thessalonians*. NICNT. Grand Rapids: Eerdmans, 2009.

———. *God's Empowering Presence: The Holy Spirit in the Letters of Paul*. Peabody, MA: Hendrickson, 1994.

———. *Pauline Christology: An Exegetical-Theological Study*. Peabody, MA: Hendrickson, 2007.

———. *Paul's Letter to the Philippians*. NICNT. Grand Rapids: Eerdmans, 1995.

———. *1 and 2 Timothy, Titus*. NIBCNT 13. Peabody, MA: Hendrickson, 1988.

Finlan, Stephen. *The Apostle Paul and the Pauline Tradition*. Collegeville, MN: Liturgical, 2008.

———. *The Background and Content of Paul's Cultic Atonement Metaphors*. SBLAbib 19. Atlanta: Society of Biblical Literature, 2004.

Fitzmyer, Joseph A. *The Letter to Philemon: A New Translation with Introduction and Commentary*. AB 34C. New York: Doubleday, 2000.

Fowl, Stephen E. *Philippians*. The Two Horizons New Testament Commentary. Grand Rapids: Eerdmans, 2005.

———. *The Story of Christ in the Ethics of Paul: An Analysis of the Function of the Hymnic Material in the Pauline Corpus*. JSNTSup 36. Sheffield: JSOT, 1990.

Garland, David E. *Colossians and Philemon: The NIV Application Commentary*. Grand Rapids: Zondervan, 1998.

———. *1 Corinthians*. BECNT. Grand Rapids: Baker, 2003.

———. "Philippians." In *The Expositor's Bible Commentary: Revised Edition*, edited by Tremper Longman and David E. Garland, 12:177–261. Grand Rapids: Zondervan, 2006.

Gaventa, Beverly Roberts. *Our Mother Saint Paul*. Louisville: Westminster John Knox, 2007.

Gillman, John. "A Thematic Comparison: 1 Cor 15:50–57 and 2 Cor 5:1–5." *JBL* 107 (1988) 439–54.

Goodwin, Mark J. *Paul, Apostle of the Living God: Kerygma and Conversion in 2 Corinthians*. Harrisburg, PA: Trinity, 2001.

———. "The Pauline Background of the Living God as Interpretive Context for 1 Timothy 4.10." *JSNT* 61 (1996) 65–85.

Gorman, Michael J. *Apostle of the Crucified Lord: A Theological Introduction to Paul and His Letters*. Grand Rapids: Eerdmans, 2004.

Green, Gene L. *The Letters to the Thessalonians*. Pillar New Testament Commentary. Grand Rapids: Eerdmans, 2002.

Hansen, G. Walter. *The Letter to the Philippians*. Pillar New Testament Commentary. Grand Rapids: Eerdmans, 2009.

Harland, Philip A. "House Church." In *The New Interpreter's Dictionary of the Bible*, 2:903. Nashville: Abingdon, 2007.

Harrington, Daniel J. "Christians and Jews in Colossians." In *Diaspora Jews and Judaism: Essays in Honor of, and in Dialogue with, A. Thomas Kraabel*, edited by J. Andrew Overmann and Robert S. MacLennan, 153–61. South Florida Studies in the History of Judaism 41. Atlanta: Scholars, 1992.

Harris, Murray J. *Colossians & Philemon*. Exegetical Guide to the Greek New Testament. Grand Rapids: Eerdmans, 1991.

———. *The Second Epistle to the Corinthians: A Commentary on the Greek Text*. NIGTC. Grand Rapids: Eerdmans, 2005.

Harrison, James R. *Paul's Language of Grace in Its Graeco-Roman Context*. WUNT 172. Tübingen: Mohr/Siebeck, 2003.

Heil, John Paul. "The Chiastic Structure and Meaning of Paul's Letter to Philemon." *Bib* 82 (2001) 178–206.

———. *Colossians: Encouragement to Walk in All Wisdom as Holy Ones in Christ*. SBLECL 4. Atlanta: Society of Biblical Literature, 2010.

———. "Ephesians 5:18b: 'But Be Filled in the Spirit.'" *CBQ* 69 (2007) 506–16.

———. *Ephesians: Empowerment to Walk in Love for the Unity of All in Christ*. Studies in Biblical Literature 13. Atlanta: Society of Biblical Literature, 2007.

———. *Paul's Letter to the Romans: A Reader-Response Commentary*. New York: Paulist, 1987.

———. *Philippians: Let Us Rejoice in Being Conformed to Christ*. SBLECL 3. Atlanta: Society of Biblical Literature, 2010.

———. *The Rhetorical Role of Scripture in 1 Corinthians*. Studies in Biblical Literature 15. Atlanta: Society of Biblical Literature, 2005.

———. *Romans—Paul's Letter of Hope*. AnBib 112. Rome: Biblical Institute, 1987.

———. "Those Now 'Asleep' (Not Dead) Must Be 'Awakened' for the Day of the Lord in 1 Thess 5.9–10." *NTS* 46 (2000) 464–71.

———. "The Voices of Scripture and Paul's Rhetorical Strategy of Hope in Romans 15:7–13." *Theoforum* 33 (2002) 187–211.

Ho, Chiao Ek. "Mission in the Pastoral Epistles." In *Entrusted with the Gospel: Paul's Theology in the Pastoral Epistles*, edited by Andreas J. Köstenberger and Terry L. Wilder, 241–67. Nashville: Broadman & Holman, 2010.

Hock, Andreas. "Christ Is the Parade: A Comparative Study of the Triumphal Procession in 2 Cor 2,14 and Col 2,15." *Bib* 88 (2007) 110–19.

Hoehner, Harold W. *Ephesians: An Exegetical Commentary*. Grand Rapids: Baker, 2002.

Hollander, Harm W., and Joost Holleman. "The Relationship of Death, Sin, and Law in 1 Cor 15:56." *NovT* 35 (1993) 270–91.

Hooker, Morna D. "Were There False Teachers in Colossae?" In *Christ and Spirit in the New Testament: Essays in Honour of Charles Francis Digby Moule*, edited by Barnabas Lindars and Stephen S. Smalley, 315–31. Cambridge: Cambridge University Press, 1973.

Hurtado, Larry W. *At the Origins of Christian Worship: The Context and Character of Earliest Christian Devotion*. Grand Rapids: Eerdmans, 1999.

———. "The Doxology at the End of Romans." In *New Testament Textual Criticism: Its Significance for Exegesis: Essays in Honor of Bruce M. Metzger*, edited by Eldon Jay Epp and Gordon D. Fee, 185–99. Oxford: Clarendon, 1981.

———. *How on Earth Did Jesus Become a God?: Historical Questions about Earliest Devotion to Jesus*. Grand Rapids: Eerdmans, 2005.

———. *Lord Jesus Christ: Devotion to Jesus in Earliest Christianity*. Grand Rapids: Eerdmans, 2003.

———. "Worship, NT Christian." In *The New Interpreter's Dictionary of the Bible*, 5:910–23. Nashville: Abingdon, 2009.

Jeal, Roy R. *Integrating Theology and Ethics in Ephesians: The Ethos of Communication*. Studies in Bible and Early Christianity 43. Lewiston, NY: Mellen, 2000.

Jewett, Robert. "Paul, Phoebe, and the Spanish Mission." In *The Social World of Formative Christianity and Judaism: Essays in Tribute to Howard Clark Kee*, edited by Jacob Neusner et al., 144–64. Philadelphia: Fortress, 1988.

———. *Romans: A Commentary*. Hermeneia. Minneapolis: Fortress, 2007.

Johnson, Andy. "The Sanctification of the Imagination in 1 Thessalonians." In *Holiness and Ecclesiology in the New Testament*, edited by Kent E. Brower and Andy Johnson, 275–92. Grand Rapids: Eerdmans, 2007.

Johnson, Luke Timothy. *The First and Second Letters to Timothy: A New Translation with Introduction and Commentary*. AB 35A. New York: Doubleday, 2001.

———. *Religious Experience in Earliest Christianity: A Missing Dimension in New Testament Study*. Minneapolis: Fortress, 1998.

———. *The Writings of the New Testament: Third Edition*. Minneapolis: Fortress, 2010.

Joubert, Stephan J. "Religious Reciprocity in 2 Corinthians 9:6–15: Generosity and Gratitude as Legitimate Responses to the *charis tou theou*." *Neot* 33 (1999) 79–90.

Kellermann, Ulrich. "*aphorizō*." In *EDNT* 1:183–84.

Kiley, Mark. *Colossians as Pseudepigraphy*. The Biblical Seminar 4. Sheffield: JSOT, 1986.

Klassen, William. "The Sacred Kiss in the New Testament: An Example of Social Boundary Lines." *NTS* 39 (1993) 122–35.

Knight, George W. *The Pastoral Epistles: A Commentary on the Greek Text*. NIGTC. Grand Rapids: Eerdmans, 1992.

Köstenberger, Andreas J. "Ascertaining Women's God-Ordained Roles: An Interpretation of 1 Timothy 2:15." *BBR* 7 (1997) 107–44.

———. "Hermeneutical and Exegetical Challenges in Interpreting the Pastoral Epistles." In *Entrusted with the Gospel: Paul's Theology in the Pastoral Epistles*, edited by Andreas J. Köstenberger and Terry L. Wilder, 1–27. Nashville: Broadman & Holman, 2010.

Lampe, Peter. *Die städtrömischen Christen in den ersten beiden Jahrhunderten.* WUNT 2/18. Tübingen: Mohr, 1987.

Lanci, John R. *A New Temple for Corinth: Rhetorical and Archaeological Approaches to Pauline Imagery.* Studies in Biblical Literature 1. New York: Lang, 1997.

Lieu, Judith M. "'Grace to You and Peace': The Apostolic Greeting." *BJRL* 68 (1985) 161–78.

Lincoln, Andrew T. *Ephesians.* WBC 42. Dallas: Word, 1990.

Lyons, George. "Church and Holiness in Ephesians." In *Holiness and Ecclesiology in the New Testament,* edited by Kent E. Brower and Andy Johnson, 238–56. Grand Rapids: Eerdmans, 2007.

Madsen, Thorvald B. "The Ethics of the Pastoral Epistles." In *Entrusted with the Gospel: Paul's Theology in the Pastoral Epistles,* edited by Andreas J. Köstenberger and Terry L. Wilder, 219–40. Nashville: Broadman & Holman, 2010.

Malan, Francois S. "Church Singing According to the Pauline Epistles." *Neot* 32 (1998) 509–24.

Malherbe, Abraham J. *The Letters to the Thessalonians: A New Translation with Introduction and Commentary.* AB 32B. New York: Doubleday, 2000.

Marshall, I. Howard. *The Pastoral Epistles.* ICC. Edinburgh: T. & T. Clark, 1999.

Martens, M. P. "First Corinthians 7:14: 'Sanctified' by the Believing Spouse." *Notes* 10 (1996) 31–35.

Martin, Troy W. "Circumcision in Galatia and the Holiness of God's Ecclesiae." In *Holiness and Ecclesiology in the New Testament,* edited by Kent E. Brower and Andy Johnson, 219–37. Grand Rapids: Eerdmans, 2007.

Martyn, J. Louis. *Galatians.* AB 33A. New York: Doubleday, 1998.

Matera, Frank J. *II Corinthians: A Commentary.* NTL. Louisville: Westminster John Knox, 2003.

———. "Galatians, Letter to the." In *Eerdmans Dictionary of the Bible,* edited by David Noel Freedman, 476–78. Grand Rapids: Eerdmans, 2000.

———. *New Testament Theology: Exploring Diversity and Unity.* Louisville: Westminster John Knox, 2007.

———. *Romans.* Paideia Commentaries on the New Testament. Grand Rapids: Baker, 2010.

Matthews, Victor H. "Clothe Oneself, To." In *The New Interpreter's Dictionary of the Bible,* 1:696. Nashville: Abingdon, 2006.

McBride, S. Dean. "Bless." In *The New Interpreter's Dictionary of the Bible,* 1:476–77, Nashville: Abingdon, 2007.

Merkle, Benjamin L. "Ecclesiology in the Pastoral Epistles." In *Entrusted with the Gospel: Paul's Theology in the Pastoral Epistles,* edited by Andreas J. Köstenberger and Terry L. Wilder, 173–98. Nashville: Broadman & Holman, 2010.

Metzger, Bruce Manning. *A Textual Commentary on the Greek New Testament.* 2nd ed. Stuttgart: Deutsche Bibelgesellschaft, 1994.

Mitchell, Margaret M. *Paul and the Rhetoric of Reconciliation: An Exegetical Investigation of the Language and Composition of 1 Corinthians.* HUT 28. Tübingen: Mohr, 1991.

———. "Corrective Composition, Corrective Exegesis: The Teaching on Prayer in 1 Tim 2,1–15." In *1 Timothy Reconsidered,* edited by Karl Paul Donfried, 41–62. Colloquium Oecumenicum Paulinum 18. Leuven: Peeters, 2008.

Mitchell, Nathan D. "Paul's Eucharistic Theology." *Worship* 83 (2009) 250–62.

Moo, Douglas J. *The Letters to Colossians and to Philemon.* Pillar New Testament Commentary. Grand Rapids: Eerdmans, 2008.

Mounce, William D. *The Pastoral Epistles.* WBC 46. Nashville: Nelson, 2000.

Muddiman, John. *A Commentary on the Epistle to the Ephesians.* BNTC. London: Continuum, 2001.

Murphy-O'Connor, Jerome. "2 Timothy Contrasted with 1 Timothy and Titus." *RB* 98 (1991) 403–18.

Newman, Carey C. *Paul's Glory Christology: Tradition and Rhetoric.* NovTSup. Leiden: Brill, 1992.

Newton, Michael. *The Concept of Purity at Qumran and in the Letters of Paul.* SNTSMS 53. Cambridge: Cambridge University Press, 1985.

Neyrey, Jerome H. *Give God the Glory: Ancient Prayer and Worship in Cultural Perspective.* Grand Rapids: Eerdmans, 2007.

———. "Lost in Translation: Did It Matter If Christians 'Thanked' God or 'Gave God Glory'?" *CBQ* 71 (2009) 1–23.

Nicholl, Colin R. *From Hope to Despair in Thessalonica: Situating 1 and 2 Thessalonians.* SNTSMS 126. Cambridge: Cambridge University Press, 2004.

Nicholson, Suzanne. *Dynamic Oneness: The Significance and Flexibility of Paul's One-God Language.* Eugene, OR: Pickwick, 2010.

Nolland, John. "Grace as Power." *NovT* 28 (1986) 26–31.

O'Brien, Peter Thomas. *The Epistle to the Philippians: A Commentary on the Greek Text.* NIGTC. Grand Rapids: Eerdmans, 1991.

———. *Introductory Thanksgivings in the Letters of Paul.* NovTSup 49. Leiden: Brill, 1977.

———. *The Letter to the Ephesians.* Pillar New Testament Commentary. Grand Rapids: Eerdmans, 1999.

Oakes, Peter. "Made Holy by the Holy Spirit: Holiness and Ecclesiology in Romans." In *Holiness and Ecclesiology in the New Testament,* edited by Kent E. Brower and Andy Johnson, 167–83. Grand Rapids: Eerdmans, 2007.

———. *Philippians: From People to Letter.* SNTSMS 110. Cambridge: Cambridge University Press, 2001.

———. *Reading Romans in Pompeii: Paul's Letter at Ground Level.* Minneapolis: Fortress, 2009.

Patsch, Hermann. "*eulogeō.*" In *EDNT* 2:79–80.

Penn, Michael Philip. *Kissing Christians: Ritual and Community in the Late Ancient Church.* Divinations. Philadelphia: University of Pennsylvania Press, 2005.

———. "Performing Family: Ritual Kissing and the Construction of Early Christian Kinship." *JECS* 10 (2002) 151–74.

Peterson, David G. *Engaging with God: A Biblical Theology of Worship.* Downers Grove, IL: InterVarsity, 1992.

Phillips, Thomas E. *Paul, His Letters, and Acts.* Library of Pauline Studies. Peabody, MA: Hendrickson, 2009.

Pickett, Raymond. *The Cross in Corinth: The Social Significance of the Death of Jesus.* JSNTSup 143. Sheffield: Sheffield Academic, 1997.

Pilhofer, Peter. *Philippi: Die erste christliche Gemeinde Europas.* WUNT 87. Tübingen: Mohr/Siebeck, 1995.

Bibliography

Powell, Mark Allan. "Worship, New Testament." In *Eerdmans Dictionary of the Bible*, edited by David Noel Freedman, 1391–92. Grand Rapids: Eerdmans, 2000.

Powery, Emerson B. "Kiss." In *The New Interpreter's Dictionary of the Bible*, 3:536. Nashville: Abingdon, 2008.

Prior, Michael. *Paul the Letter-Writer and the Second Letter to Timothy*. JSNTSup 23. Sheffield: JSOT, 1989.

Reicke, Bo. "The Historical Setting of Colossians." *RevExp* 70 (1973) 429–38.

———. *Re-Examining Paul's Letters: The History of the Pauline Correspondence*. Harrisburg, PA: Trinity, 2001.

Richards, E. Randolph. *Paul and First-Century Letter Writing: Secretaries, Composition and Collection*. Downers Grove, IL: InterVarsity, 2004.

Riesner, Rainer. "Once More: Luke-Acts and the Pastoral Epistles." In *History and Exegesis: New Testament Essays in Honor of Dr. E. Earle Ellis for His 80th Birthday*, edited by Sang-Won Son, 239–58. London: T. & T. Clark, 2006.

Robinson, John A. T. *Redating the New Testament*. London: SCM, 1976.

Roloff, Jürgen. "*ekklēsia*." In *EDNT* 1:410–15.

Romaniuk, Kazimierz. "Was Phoebe in Romans 16,1 a Deaconess?" *ZNW* 81 (1990) 132–34.

Rosen, Leora Nadine. "Temple and Holiness in 1 Corinthians 5." *TynBul* 42 (1991) 137–45.

Rosscup, James E. "The Importance of Prayer in Ephesians." *Master's Seminary Journal* 6 (1995) 57–78.

Sandnes, Karl Olav. "Prophecy—A Sign for Believers (1 Cor 14,20–25)." *Bib* 77 (1996) 1–15.

Sappington, Thomas J. *Revelation and Redemption at Colossae*. JSNTSup 53. Sheffield: JSOT, 1991.

Schnabel, Eckhard J. *Paul the Missionary: Realities, Strategies and Methods*. Downers Grove, IL: InterVarsity, 2008.

Schubert, Paul. *Form and Function of the Pauline Thanksgiving*. BZNW 20. Berlin: Töpelmann, 1939.

Schulz, Ray R. "A Case for 'President' Phoebe in Romans 16:2." *Lutheran Journal of Theology* 24 (1990) 124–27.

Silva, Moisés. *Philippians*. BECNT. Grand Rapids: Baker, 2005.

Smith, Craig A. *Timothy's Task, Paul's Prospect: A New Reading of 2 Timothy*. NTM 12. Sheffield: Sheffield Phoenix, 2006.

Smith, Ian K. *Heavenly Perspective: A Study of the Apostle Paul's Response to a Jewish Mystical Movement at Colossae*. LNTS 326. London: T. & T. Clark, 2006.

Snodgrass, Klyne R. *Ephesians: The NIV Application Commentary*. Grand Rapids: Zondervan, 1996.

Soards, Marion. "Galatians, Letter to the." In *The New Interpreter's Dictionary of the Bible*, 2:508–14. Nashville: Abingdon, 2007.

Spicq, Ceslas. *Saint Paul: Les Épîtres Pastorales*. 4th ed. 2 vols. EBib. Paris: Gabalda, 1969.

———. *Theological Lexicon of the New Testament*. Translated and edited by James D. Ernest. 3 vols. Peabody, MA: Hendrickson, 1994.

Standhartinger, Angela. "*Eusebeia* in den Pastoralbriefen: Ein Beitrag zum Einfluss römischen Denkens auf das Entstehende Christentum." *NovT* 48 (2006) 51–82.

Stegman, Thomas D. *Second Corinthians*. Catholic Commentary on Sacred Scripture. Grand Rapids: Baker, 2009.

Stettler, Christian. "The Opponents at Colossae." In *Paul and His Opponents*, edited by Stanley E. Porter, 169–200. Pauline Studies 2. Leiden: Brill, 2005.

Stirewalt, Luther M. *Paul: The Letter Writer*. Grand Rapids: Eerdmans, 2003.

Suggit, John N. "The Fatherhood of God: Galatians 1:3." *Neot* 37 (2003) 97–103.

Sumney, Jerry L. *Colossians: A Commentary*. NTL. Louisville: Westminster John Knox, 2008.

Taylor, Joan E. "Baptism." In *The New Interpreter's Dictionary of the Bible*, 1:390–95. Nashville: Abingdon, 2006.

Thiselton, Anthony C. *The First Epistle to the Corinthians: A Commentary on the Greek Text*. NIGTC. Grand Rapids: Eerdmans, 2000.

Thompson, Marianne Meye. *Colossians and Philemon*. The Two Horizons New Testament Commentary. Grand Rapids: Eerdmans, 2005.

Thurston, Bonnie B., and Judith M. Ryan. *Philippians and Philemon*. SP 10. Collegeville, MN: Liturgical, 2005.

Tipei, John Fleter. *The Laying on of Hands in the New Testament: Its Significance, Techniques, and Effects*. Lanham, MD: University Press of America, 2009.

Tomlinson, F. Alan. "'The Purpose and Stewardship Theme Within the Pastoral Epistles." In *Entrusted with the Gospel: Paul's Theology in the Pastoral Epistles*, edited by Andreas J. Köstenberger and Terry L. Wilder, 52–83. Nashville: Broadman & Holman, 2010.

Towner, Philip H. "The Function of the Public Reading of Scripture in 1 Tim 4:13 and in the Biblical Tradition." *Southern Baptist Journal of Theology* 7 (2003) 44–54.

———. *The Letters to Timothy and Titus*. NICNT. Grand Rapids: Eerdmans, 2006.

Trebilco, Paul R. *The Early Christians in Ephesus from Paul to Ignatius*. Grand Rapids: Eerdmans, 2004.

Usami, Kôshi. *Somatic Comprehension of Unity: The Church in Ephesus*. AnBib 101. Rome: Biblical Institute, 1983.

Vahrenhorst, Martin. *Kultische Sprache in den Paulusbriefen*. WUNT 230. Tübingen: Mohr/Siebeck, 2008.

Van Voorst, Robert E. "Why Is There No Thanksgiving Period in Galatians?: An Assessement of an Exegetical Commonplace." *JBL* 129 (2010) 153–72.

Wagner, J. Ross. "Working Out Salvation: Holiness and Community in Philippians." In *Holiness and Ecclesiology in the New Testament*, edited by Kent E. Brower and Andy Johnson, 257–74. Grand Rapids: Eerdmans, 2007.

Walton, Steve. "Titus." In *The New Interpreter's Dictionary of the Bible*, 5:609. Nashville: Abingdon, 2009.

Wansink, Craig S. *Chained in Christ: The Experience and Rhetoric of Paul's Imprisonments*. JSNTSup 130. Sheffield: Sheffield Academic, 1996.

Ware, James P. *The Mission of the Church in Paul's Letter to the Philippians in the Context of Ancient Judaism*. NovTSup 120. Leiden: Brill, 2005.

Webster's New World Dictionary. New York: Simon and Schuster, 1984.

Weima, Jeffrey A. D. *Neglected Endings: The Significance of the Pauline Letter Closings*. JSNTSup 101. Sheffield: JSOT, 1994.

Wevers, John William. *Notes on the Greek Text of Numbers*. SBLSCS 46. Atlanta: Scholars, 1998.

Whelan, Caroline F. "Amica Pauli: The Role of Phoebe in the Early Church." *JSNT* 49 (1993) 67–85.

Whitlark, Jason A. "Enabling *Charis*: Transformation of the Convention of Reciprocity by Philo and in Ephesians." *PRSt* 30 (2003) 325–57.

Wieland, George M. "The Function of Salvation in the Letters to Timothy and Titus." In *Entrusted with the Gospel: Paul's Theology in the Pastoral Epistles*, edited by Andreas J. Köstenberger and Terry L. Wilder, 153–72. Nashville: Broadman & Holman, 2010.

———. "Roman Crete and the Letter to Titus." *NTS* 55 (2009) 338–54.

———. *The Significance of Salvation: A Study of Salvation Language in the Pastoral Epistles.* Paternoster Biblical Monographs. Milton Keynes, UK: Paternoster, 2006.

Wilder, Terry L. *Pseudonymity, the New Testament and Deception: An Inquiry into Intention and Reception.* Lanham: University Press of America, 2004.

———. "Pseudonymity, the New Testament, and the Pastoral Epistles." In *Entrusted with the Gospel: Paul's Theology in the Pastoral Epistles*, edited by Andreas J. Köstenberger and Terry L. Wilder, 28–51. Nashville: Broadman & Holman, 2010.

Wiles, Gordon P. *Paul's Intercessory Prayers: The Significance of the Intercessory Prayer Passages in the Letters of St. Paul.* SNTSMS 24. Cambridge: Cambridge University Press, 1974.

Wilson, Robert McLachlan. *Colossians and Philemon.* ICC. London: T. & T. Clark, 2005.

Winter, Bruce W. "Carnal Conduct and Sanctification in 1 Corinthians: *Simul Sanctus et Peccator?*" In *Holiness and Ecclesiology in the New Testament*, edited by Kent E. Brower and Andy Johnson, 184–200. Grand Rapids: Eerdmans, 2007.

———. *Roman Wives, Roman Widows: The Appearance of New Women and the Pauline Communities.* Grand Rapids: Eerdmans, 2003.

Witherington, Ben. *Friendship and Finances in Philippi: The Letter of Paul to the Philippians.* Valley Forge: Trinity, 1994.

———. *Grace in Galatia: A Commentary on Paul's Letter to the Galatians.* Grand Rapids: Eerdmans, 1998.

———. *Letters and Homilies for Hellenized Christians.* Vol. 1: *A Socio-Rhetorical Commentary on Titus, 1–2 Timothy and 1–3 John.* Downers Grove, IL: InterVarsity, 2006.

———. *1 and 2 Thessalonians: A Socio-Rhetorical Commentary.* Grand Rapids: Eerdmans, 2006.

Wolfe, B. Paul. "The Sagacious Use of Scripture." In *Entrusted with the Gospel: Paul's Theology in the Pastoral Epistles*, edited by Andreas J. Köstenberger and Terry L. Wilder, 199–218. Nashville: Broadman & Holman, 2010.

Wright, Nicholas Thomas. *The Epistles of Paul to the Colossians and Philemon: An Introduction and Commentary.* TNTC. Grand Rapids: Eerdmans, 1986.

Yee, Tet-Lim N. *Jews, Gentiles and Ethnic Reconciliation: Paul's Jewish Identity and Ephesians.* SNTSMS 130. Cambridge: Cambridge University Press, 2005.

Zoccali, Christopher. "'And So All Israel Will Be Saved': Competing Interpretations of Romans 11.26 in Pauline Scholarship." *JSNT* 30 (2008) 289–318.

Scripture Index

Author Index

Author Index

Made in the USA
San Bernardino, CA
03 January 2014